ASTD Training Basics Series

ASTD Training Basics Series

PRESENTATION Basics

ROBERT J. ROSANIA

A Complete, How-to
Guide to Help You:

◉ Present Like a Pro, Even If You're Not

◉ Prepare and Deliver a Credible Presentation

◉ Choose the Right Presentation Tools

ASTD
*Linking People,
Learning & Performance*

ASTD Press is an internationally renowned source of insightful and practical information on workplace learning and performance topics, including training basics, evaluation and return-on-investment (ROI), instructional systems development (ISD), e-learning, leadership, and career development.

Ordering information: Books published by ASTD Press can be purchased by visiting our Website at store.astd.org or by calling 800.628.2783 or 703.683.8100.

Library of Congress Control Number: 2003107796

ISBN: 1-56286-347-9

Acquisitions and Development Editor: Mark Morrow
Copyeditor: Karen Eddleman
Interior Design and Production: Kathleen Schaner
Cover Design: Ana Ilieva
Cover Illustration: Phil and Jim Bliss

Table of Contents

About the
Training Basics Series

ASTD's *Training Basics* series recognizes and, in some ways, celebrates the fast-paced, ever-changing reality of organizations today. Jobs, roles, and expectations change quickly. One day you might be a network administrator or a process line manager, and the next day you might be asked to train 50 employees in basic computer skills or to instruct line workers in quality processes.

Where do you turn for help? The ASTD *Training Basics* series is designed to be your one-stop solution. The series takes a minimalist approach to your learning curve dilemma and presents only the information you need to be successful. Each book in the series guides you through key aspects of training: giving presentations, making the transition to the role of trainer, designing and delivering training, and evaluating training. The books in the series also include some advanced skills such as performance and basic business proficiencies.

The ASTD *Training Basics* series is the perfect tool for training and performance professionals looking for easy-to-understand materials that will prepare non-trainers to take on a training role. In addition, this series is the perfect reference tool for any trainer's bookshelf and a quick way to hone your existing skills. The titles currently planned for the series include:

- ▶ *Presentation Basics* (2003)
- ▶ *Training Basics* (2003)
- ▶ *Design Basics* (2003)
- ▶ *Facilitation Basics* (2004).

Preface

■ ■

Have you ever sat in an audience watching a presenter and thought, "How can anyone stand up before a group, knowing all eyes are on him or her and give a presentation, yet look so at ease and composed?" After all, it's a pretty frightening notion to think that everyone is listening to each word you say and watching every move you make.

For most people, giving a presentation ranks right up there with things they fear the most. This fact is especially true for novice presenters or those who only present occasionally. I wrote this book to take the fear out of making a presentation or, at the very least, to make the experience one that will be enjoyable as well as enriching.

As a trainer I have made hundreds of presentations to groups large and small, so much of what I write about in this book is based on my experience and observation. I know what it's like to hit a home run, and I know what it's like to fall flat on my face. What I've learned throughout the years is that *anyone* can make an effective presentation as long as he or she is prepared, credible, and professional. This book gives you a simple process that you can use to prepare your presentation and equips you with the skills and techniques to help you look and sound professional.

I wrote this book both to coach you as a new presenter and to encourage you to meet the challenge of making presentations head on. You won't find anything in this book difficult to understand or hard to do. In fact, by the time you finish this book you'll be able to stand before any group feeling confident and competent, ready to meet your audience's needs, knowing you're prepared and set to go.

It is with love that I dedicate this book to my wife, Vera Regoli, whose sense of grace and compassion is a source of inspiration to me, and to my son, Aaron, whom I grow more proud of each day. I offer loving thanks to Louise and Al Rosania and to Gloria Collins for their support and guidance. I also extend my appreciation to Kay Steinkirchner and Maribeth Renne and my colleagues at Manchester for giving me the opportunity to be part of their team. Profound thanks are due Angela McGlynn for teaching me the meaning of true friendship. Finally, I wish to honor Rip Collins, who touched so many and whose memory will remain with me always.

Robert J. Rosania
July 2003

Presentation: A Critical Skill

▪▪▪▪▪▪▪▪▪▪▪▪▪▪▪▪▪▪▪▪▪▪▪▪▪▪▪▪▪▪▪▪▪▪▪

 What's Inside This Chapter

Here, you'll see how to:

▶ Use this book to help you become a successful presenter
▶ Become a prepared and credible presenter
▶ Locate information in this book using a chapter-by-chapter outline
▶ Use the icons as a guide to special material in this book

How *Presentation Basics* Can Help You

Making a presentation is not a walk in the park for most people. The thought of speaking in front of a group is stressful, if not downright incapacitating. In fact, we've all read the surveys that put presenting before a group near the top of every list of things people fear most. Many new training practitioners and subject matter experts (SMEs) are expected to make great presentations without the basic tools of the craft. The good news is that it is possible to learn how to make a presentation and maybe even enjoy the experience.

That's what this book is all about—preparing you to shine in front of a group. The concepts presented in this book are not complicated or hard to understand. In fact, as the name of this series implies, this is a basic book about the art of effective presentations. Use this book if you are a

- ▶ subject matter expert asked to share your knowledge about a new product line with your colleagues
- ▶ team leader responsible for training team members to implement a new work process
- ▶ novice training practitioner about to introduce a training module to improve performance
- ▶ new manager asked to share your plans for a division
- ▶ beginning salesperson looking to influence organizational decision makers.

What You Can Expect to Learn

Your success depends on your developing an effective presentation process to follow and your development of the right skills and techniques to support your unique process. Once you are comfortable with the basic mechanics of effective presentations, your stress and fear can be eliminated or at least reduced greatly. An effective presenter is credible, is well prepared, uses tried and true tools, and has a grasp of the basic presentation skills you'll learn in this book. In addition, an effective presenter pays attention to and is prepared for the little (and sometimes not so little) things that happen to every presenter at one time or another, such as last-minute room set-up changes or audiovisual glitches.

As you explore this book, you'll see that being a good presenter is not as difficult as you might think. It's all a matter of your approach and attitude. Rather than dreading the experience, try thinking of it as an opportunity. Here are four reasons to feel good about making a presentation:

1. You have an opportunity to make a small difference in the lives of each person you touch.
2. It's a wonderful opportunity to express yourself and build self-esteem and confidence.
3. It gives you a chance to showcase your knowledge, skills, and abilities in a professional way.
4. It provides you with a tremendous feeling of accomplishment when it's done.

If you think about it, it's pretty hard to be credible if you're unprepared, or vice versa for that matter. So just assume that if you have one (prepared), you will have the other (credibility). Think about this: Your audience will know in an instant if you are not prepared to give your presentation, so there's no easy way to hide it. Even if your presentation is less than perfect, your audience will give you the benefit of the doubt if it believes you were prepared and did your best.

What Does Credibility Mean?

Being credible is mostly about perception. Credibility is more than just showing up and dazzling an audience. It's about honesty, believability, and passion for what you are presenting. If you score big here, you're on your way to a successful presentation. But, perception can make the difference between success and failure.

You'll recognize the importance of credibility, and you'll see this concept come up time and again as you go through this book. Credibility is not only about your knowledge of the subject you are presenting, but it is also about the confidence you exhibit and the respect you have for your audience.

Being Prepared

Being prepared is a little less subjective. An audience usually knows when a presenter is prepared. The message is clear, the transitions are crisp, and the audience clearly understands WIIFM ("What's in it for me?"). Of course, audiences are usually able to pick up when the opposite is true, too. For example, if the presenter has to read from a script, has difficulty answering basic level questions, cannot operate an overhead projector, or fumbles with a laptop computer tied to a projector, it is clear the presenter is unprepared. Even poor slides or clumsy use of a flipchart indicates a presenter who is unprepared.

Basic Rule 1
If you are prepared, you'll be credible!

Chapter-by-Chapter Highlights

This book uses the term *presentation* to represent a range of situations from one-on-one training to an informational seminar offered to a small group to a speech delivered to 200 people. Differences obviously exist in how you might prepare and present for each of these kinds of situations, but, as you will see, the techniques are very similar. Here's a summary of the nine chapters in *Presentation Basics:*

▶ *Chapter 1—Presentation: A Critical Skill.* The chapter you are reading gives you an overview of the book and explains how to take advantage of the basic presentation principles offered. It establishes the premise that the success of any presenter is based on being prepared and credible. The chapter also describes the icons used in this book and how these icons will help you get the most out of the information provided.

▶ *Chapter 2—Be Prepared to Succeed.* Careful preparation is an absolute requirement for any successful presentation. This chapter introduces some important presentation basics, as well as six easy-to-follow steps guaranteed to make every presentation a successful one.

▶ *Chapter 3—Getting Ready to Deliver Your Presentation.* Once you're prepared, it's time to deliver! This chapter takes the mystery out of developing a style that fits you and teaches you the most effective skills and techniques to use in your presentation. It also provides ways of relieving the anxiety that comes with making any presentation.

▶ *Chapter 4—The Art of Facilitation.* Becoming an effective facilitator can take your presentations to a higher level. The art of good facilitation requires that you know when and how to ask the right questions and what it takes to create an atmosphere that fosters great discussions. This chapter can help you become a more skillful facilitator as you begin to incorporate more facilitation into your presentations.

▶ *Chapter 5—Setting the Right Environment.* Paying attention to the details is what often separates a good presentation from a great one. In this chapter you will see how to set the right environment for your presentation by making the right choices of room size and arrangement, determining the proper setup of audiovisual support, and managing the minor interruptions that can affect any presentation.

▶ *Chapter 6—Choosing and Using Audiovisual Aids.* People remember more of what they see than what they hear. That's why choosing the right audiovisual aids can make or break a presentation. This chapter not only provides the basics, it goes into some details that can help you choose and use the audiovisual aids commonly used by new and experienced presenters.

▶ *Chapter 7—When Things Go Wrong.* How can you handle disruptive or even unruly audience members? What do you do if you draw a blank in the middle of your presentation? Preventing problems is always the best road to take, but what happens when things go wrong even when you've done all you could to make things right? This chapter suggests some ways to handle the most common problems presenters encounter.

▶ *Chapter 8—Improving Your Skills.* Smart presenters work to improve their craft. This chapter offers 20 practical actions you can take now to further your development as an effective presenter.

▶ *Chapter 9—Where to Get More Information.* This chapter presents an extensive bibliography of the many written and technology-driven publications available to help you become a more effective presenter.

Icons to Guide You

This book strives to make it as easy as possible for you to understand and apply its lessons. Icons throughout the book help you identify key points that can mean the difference between a successful presentation and an embarrassing one.

What's Inside This Chapter

Each chapter opens with a short list—really a quick access guide—to introduce you to the rest of the chapter. If you are reading this book, you're probably in a hurry to get something done. You can use this section to identify the information the chapter contains and, if you wish, skip ahead to the material that will be most useful to you.

Think About This

These little helpful reminders are like extra tools in your presenter's toolkit. Think of them as an extra layer of preparation to build your presentation confidence.

Basic Rules

These rules cut to the chase. Although they are easy to remember, they are extremely important concepts for every presenter.

Noted

Sometimes a point or suggested practice needs some additional detail to help you understand the concept. Or, perhaps a little digression would be helpful to make a point. You will find these items under the "noted" icon.

Getting It Done

The final section of each chapter offers you a chance to practice some of the concepts discussed in the chapter and provides final tips and pointers to help you apply what you have learned.

Let's Go!

There is no simple prescription for making a presentation. A style and process ideal for one person might be wrong for someone else. But, there are certain constants in making a presentation, like being prepared and establishing and maintaining your credibility, as well as having a passion for your subject, that transcend style and process.

This book will help you maneuver through the morass of presentation *dos* and *don't*s and provide a practical framework for becoming an effective presenter. Because this book is for the new or less-experienced presenter, emphasis at all times is placed on taking a practical and easy-to-implement approach to presenting. As you read this book, you'll learn the importance of understanding your audience's needs, as well as the value of taking care of the details. You'll see how to prepare a presentation and the best way to deliver it. These are the essentials of making a successful presentation.

So, use what you think will work, and then practice, practice, practice. The excitement and rewards of being a presenter are just around the corner.

Be Prepared to Succeed

What's Inside This Chapter

Here, you'll see how to:

▶ Build on the elements of successful presentations
▶ Become a winning presenter using six easy steps
▶ Develop the purpose of your presentation
▶ Deal with your audience
▶ Be an expert presenter without being an expert
▶ Choose the right audiovisuals to support your presentation
▶ Close on a high note
▶ Practice to make a perfect presentation

Some presenters overprepare for their presentations; they write out every word on notecards. But, if you overscript your presentation, a single question might throw you off. Other presenters take the opposite approach to their presentations and think that they can wing it without notes because they "know" the subject. If you use no notes, though, a momentary lapse in concentration could throw your presentation into chaos because you have nothing to help you get back on track.

Naturally much of how you go about preparing depends on what kind of presentation you are going to make, how you feel about your subject, who your audience is, and what method you are most comfortable with. If you've got a way of preparing a presentation and your methods work, then go with them and use this book for some helpful tips. Most readers of this book, though, are new presenters who'll be able to seize the ideas in this book to make their preparation experience go a little easier.

Presentation Basics

Before getting into specific details about making a presentation, you should understand some of the elements common to all presentations. Think of every presentation you make as having a beginning, middle, and a closing section, just like most books you read. Audiences and readers like structure in their books and the presentations they attend. Here are the three parts spelled out more clearly:

1. The beginning grabs your audience's attention.
2. The middle provides your audience with some key ideas or skills to think about or act upon.
3. The closing enables your audience to think or perform in a different way.

That's it! You can make the process more complicated, but what's the point? Even the State of the Union address follows the same simple, successful structure: beginning, middle, closing.

Basic Rule 2
Keep it simple. Remember every book, play, song, and speech has a beginning, middle, and closing. Don't try to improve on this successful formula.

Six Steps to Winning Presentations

There are six steps guaranteed to make preparing your presentation much easier. Each step listed here is described in the sections that follow:

1. Know your purpose.
2. Know your audience and its needs.

3. Know your subject.
4. Write your presentation.
5. Choose your audiovisuals.
6. Practice, practice, and then practice some more.

Step 1: Know Your Purpose

Why should anyone be willing to sit in a room in an uncomfortable chair with a bunch of other people for an hour and listen to you? There's got to be a reason, and that's your purpose. If you want to call this an objective or a goal, that's okay, too. Call it whatever you like, just be clear in your mind why you are giving a presentation and how your audience will benefit. Failure to take these factors into account can result in frustration and, more important, a loss of credibility.

Step 2: Know Your Audience and Its Needs

Presentations are like gloves. The same glove does not fit everyone. Find out what your audience wants, and tailor your presentation to that need. A professional trainer may have a stress management workshop in a file cabinet, but it may not be appropriate for all audiences. Asking simple questions such as who the audience is, why the audience is there, and what the audience needs to know goes a long way toward making your presentation successful.

Think About This

Sometimes you'll work directly with the person who asked you to make a presentation—the sponsor. Make sure that both you and your sponsor understand why you are making a presentation. You don't want a sponsor to utter the words after your presentation, "That's not what I expected." Make sure you ask your sponsor what the audience is expected to know, be persuaded to do, or perform more effectively after your presentation. When you have the answers to these questions you then have your purpose.

Basic Rule 3

Good presenters always have a clear purpose in mind for their presentation and understand exactly what the goals are for the presentation in terms of what the audience needs to learn to do differently.

How, exactly, do you get to know your audience? After all, you're not just making this presentation *to* them; you're making it *for* them. Find out as much as you can about the audience and its needs ahead of time. Ask your sponsor about his or her perception about the audience's needs. When you begin to prepare your presentation, make sure that you adjust your language or approach for this group. If possible, you might even ask the sponsor for specific information you should include in your presentation.

Start by asking some important questions about whether the audience has any relationship to you (co-workers), how experienced your audience is in the subject matter of your presentation, and the audience's level of authority inside and outside the organization.

Relationship to You. Ask yourself if you consider the audience friends, strangers, or a little of both.

Friends usually want you to do well and can often be counted on to help out when you ask a question or you need a little support. Friends in the context of this book are simply people whom you know or who know you. They could be professional colleagues, co-workers, personal acquaintances, or any combination. Often friends can help you gain insight into the needs of the group because it's easier to approach a friend than a complete stranger. Sometimes friends are simply people eager to hear what you have to say. This is especially true for anyone who makes many presentations. Writers, those in the news, and those with authority in the organization benefit from having these kinds of friends in their audience. Use the friend factor to your advantage because you have already established credibility and trust with them.

Although you might think an audience of strangers is a tougher audience, this assumption is not necessarily correct. Those who do not know you probably assume you have something of value to say even if attendance is

Think About This

If you are presenting to a room of strangers, make a point of introducing yourself to as many attendees as possible before your presentation begins. If you get to your presentation room early enough, you can meet many attendees as they enter the room. This effort will not only make your presentation go smoother, but it will increase your credibility.

required because you are standing before them and they are sitting listening to you. Either way, don't worry too much about the stranger factor; just concentrate on getting ready for your presentation.

It's likely that very few of your presentations will be for just friends or exclusively strangers. No matter, make a point to remember to look for where your friends are in the room, because you may need to enlist their support at some point. At the same time greeting strangers as they arrive at your presentation increases your credibility and once again helps turn strangers into friends.

Your Audience's Level of Expertise. Knowing how much knowledge or expertise your audience has regarding the subject you are presenting is an important fact to know before you take the podium. An easy way to find out is simply to ask your sponsor. When preparing for your presentation ask yourself this simple question, "Does this audience really need to hear everything I am prepared to tell them?"

If your audience is new to the topic you are presenting, remember the KISS principle ("Keep it simple, stupid!"). If your audience has varied levels of experience with the topic of your presentation, try aiming your presentation approach and the material you present to the middle for informational and persuasion presentations, but adjust downward, accordingly, for training presentations to ensure that you are reaching as many people as possible.

Level of Authority. If those attending your presentation are your superiors, think of ways to involve them in the learning rather than simply telling them something. Showing this kind of respect often takes the pressure off and gives you an opportunity to win them over to your way of thinking.

Presenting to peers always has its potential pitfalls. They may perceive

Think About This

If you find yourself in a situation of making a presentation to your organizational superiors, involve your learners in the learning by asking them to share their personal experiences with a subject. Once you set up this dynamic, you are in the role of facilitator, rather than expert, which not only builds credibility but creates a less stressful atmosphere.

you, in your new role, as no longer one of them. Involve them in the learning by encouraging them to share their experiences with the subject and welcoming their suggestions, ideas, and ways of doing things. Your peers will respond more positively when they know you value their input on a subject.

When you are presenting to those you supervise or manage, it's important to remember that many presentations have gone down the tube because the presenter pulled rank. Always remember that respect is a two-way street. So, never embarrass or demean anyone in any audience—especially those who have a reporting relationship to you. Instead, try to make every presentation a learning experience and an opportunity to model the behaviors desired from your direct reports.

Noted

In her book Secrets of Power Presentations: Overcome Your Fear of Public Speaking, Build Rapport and Credibility With Your Audience, Prepare and Deliver a Dynamic Presentation *(Career Press, 2000), Micki Holliday writes, "When talking with your peers relate or share information. But be careful not to engage in one-upmanship. Draw them into the presentation and ask them to share their expertise and experience."*

Knowing who the decision makers are in an audience is important, especially with a sales or any type of persuasion presentation. The fact is not everyone in your audience is equal in the sense of decision making. Some are simply more equal than others. In these situations, it is important to gather as much information before the presentation as possible, especially around these questions:

- ▸ Who are the decision makers?
- ▸ What are their most important needs?
- ▸ What will their objections be?
- ▸ What information will they base their decision to buy or act on?

Do your best to find out this information before you present, then prepare your presentation accordingly.

Your Audience's Motivation. People come to hear presentations for several reasons. Some come to learn something new, some come for their own self-awareness, some come for training, still others come because they were told to by their boss. Somehow it all goes back to WIIFM. It's a pretty safe bet that just about the entire audience is going to be asking themselves this question. Most people are at your presentation because they perceive some value in being there. The value may be that they will learn something new, get their questions answered, learn how to perform their job better, or have an opportunity to network with other people. There is a certain enthusiasm in audiences who want to be there that you can draw from.

Just because an audience wants to be at your presentation doesn't mean that it will be easy to present to. Sometimes such audiences can be the most challenging, for example, the audience coming to hear you speak about the change in a benefits policy that may adversely affect them in some way. Even with a group like this, as you prepare, you don't have to worry much about trying to capture their attention—you've got it.

Think About This

A word of caution: Never put yourself in a position where it appears that you are only presenting to those you perceive as the decision makers. Make sure you include everyone. Sometimes individuals thought to not have much power actually do—or they may procure power in the future. Don't put all your eggs in one basket.

Put yourself in your audience's place. If the attendees are interested enough to come, they are probably interested enough to listen and learn more. As you prepare,

- ▸ anticipate the kinds of questions you will be getting
- ▸ determine how you will respond to the questions
- ▸ write out how you plan to respond
- ▸ practice your responses.

Some audiences offer a different set of challenges. These are audiences that are made up of people; some of whom have agendas different than yours. In these situations your preparation should include addressing the following issues:

- ▸ *Anticipate skepticism.* Some audiences may be wary of you or the subject you are presenting from the very beginning. In this situation, identify what you anticipate the skepticism to be and then prepare your responses with a goal to change skeptics into converts. Winning skeptics to your side often results in them becoming your greatest champions. You may have to do some research ahead of time by asking your sponsor and others in the organization to share their perceptions about what the skepticism is, who the skeptics are, and why they are skeptical. Look at skepticism as a learning experience and

Noted

You will not be able to satisfy everyone in your audience. Sometimes the best you can do is listen to an objection, acknowledge it, do your best to respond to it, and in the end move on.

an as opportunity to challenge the audience to look at both sides of an issue. Being prepared to deal with skepticism in a nondefensive way will go a long way in building credibility with your audience.

▶ *Anticipate objections.* Objections often take the form of questions. As you prepare how you will respond, ask yourself what you perceive the objections to be, whether they are based on a lack of understanding or a misperception, and if the objections follow any particular pattern (certain groups, departments, job roles). Like dealing with skepticism, objections and questions should be seen as an opportunity to express and reinforce your message, as well as a way of gaining converts to your way of thinking, if that is a goal. Objections serve as feedback that can identify areas in need of further clarification. By anticipating what objections might be raised, you further your efforts to achieve your purpose.

▶ *Anticipate indifference.* Of all the audience issues that you will have to deal with, people who are indifferent are perhaps the biggest challenge. Indifference often goes back to perceived value or, in this case, a lack of perceived value of your presentation. Of course, some people simply aren't going to budge no matter what you do or say.

Think About This

Because WIIFM is always on people's minds, try to think of reasons before your presentation why some audience members might not find value in the subject matter you are presenting. A good place to start is with your sponsor or others who are likely to be in a position to know what would create value for skeptical audience members. Use this information as a way of helping to prepare your presentation.

Audience Size. Knowing the size of the audience ahead of time will help you prepare to give your presentation. For example:

▶ *Groups of 12–15 or smaller:* This size audience allows for a much more intimate presentation and gives you the flexibility of

Basic Rule 4

Don't overlook the WIIFM principle. Give your audience plenty of reasons to pay attention. If you anticipate that there might be indifference, try to identify beforehand potential indifferent audience members, clarify possible causes of their indifference, and think about how you can appeal to what you believe is of value to them based on your research and knowledge. Remind yourself that indifference is often about issues beyond your control, so prepare as best you can, but in the end don't let it affect your presentation.

introducing group activities, exercises, and group discussions. Consider a more personal approach when preparing for this size group because you will most likely have the opportunity to connect with each member of the audience at some point during the presentation.

▶ *Groups of 15–40:* This size audience still offers some flexibility in how you present. You may still have the option of making your presentation interactive with this size audience. Remember, though, that time issues should weigh in your decision because facilitating a discussion or conducting and processing a group exercise with a group of 30 could take you well beyond your time limit.

▶ *Groups of 40–50 or larger:* In a group this size, the dynamics change pretty dramatically. With a group this large you may need some audio support, such as a microphone, for everyone to hear you. You may not have time for audience member introductions that you would in a smaller group. It certainly would not be wise to spend half of the presentation going around the room having such a large group introduce

Think About This

Professional presenters will tell you that it is much easier to prepare for any logistical breakdowns than it is for people-related issues. Your audience is always the wild card in any presentation you do. Some will hang on every word, while others will challenge you at every turn. Anticipating these people-related issues is important for your success and the reason why you must prepare and practice how you will respond to those in your audience whom you anticipate might be objectors, skeptics, or indifferent.

themselves. That's just poor planning. Of course it's more than the issues of introductions; the real issue is about planning how you will manage your time. Although groups this large don't automatically preclude some interaction in your presentation, once you start the ball rolling asking for and responding to questions, for example, it may be hard to stop.

What Does Your Audience Need to Know? Go back and examine the purpose behind your presentation. Of all the things that you can say or do in this presentation, what does your audience really need to know? Usually need-to-know material amounts to about three to five main points that may be provided by your sponsor, a senior leader, those who will be coming to the presentation, or others who can help you to understand better what your audience really needs to know as you prepare your presentation.

Basic Rule 5

It's always about your audience. Spend the time to learn about the audience's needs or else you risk missing the mark.

Step 3: Know Your Subject

Ask yourself: What do I need to know about my subject to feel competent and confident to make a presentation that will meet my audience's needs? To remove some pressure, unless you are indeed an expert on the subject you are presenting, don't think you have to act like one. Audiences will accept a presenter who is forthright about his or her expertise (or lack thereof).

One reason you spent so much time analyzing your audience was to help determine the level of understanding of the subject matter. Although you won't always have this information, try to anticipate, based on your own analysis, who will be in your audience and what level of expertise they possess. With regard to how well you know your subject, you owe your audience members five things:

1. You respect them and their needs.
2. You believe in what you say to them.
3. You are well prepared to present on the subject matter.

4. If you need to adjust your presentation to meet the needs of the audience you can and will.

5. If you don't know the answer to a question, you will get it for those who need to know as quickly as possible.

Abiding by these basic tenets helps establish an open atmosphere for learning and enhances your credibility with your audience.

You may already know as much as you need to know about your subject; if so, then you can move to step 4. If not, decide what you need to know and where to find the information. Remember, because you are in the preparation stage, do your research, and gather the information you think you will need. Don't worry initially about deciding whether what you gather will become a part of your presentation. Doing that often slows you down. Once you feel as though you have enough information, then go through it, picking and choosing the parts you think you will make use of in your presentation.

Think About This

Consider this rule of thumb: If you are training people on something they must know, gear your presentation to what you believe is somewhere toward the lowest level of understanding in your audience. You may even choose to call on some of those with more knowledge to assist you in helping the others understand. This way no one gets left behind. If you are presenting something that is good to know but not necessarily a need-to-know item, try preparing to meet the expectations of those in the midrange and above.

As for doing your research, remember not to limit yourself. Here are some places to look to do your research:

- ▶ organizational literature and material
- ▶ your sponsor
- ▶ senior leaders in the company or organization
- ▶ your manager
- ▶ the managers of those who will be in the audience
- ▶ peers or co-workers
- ▶ the Internet
- ▶ the library

> ▸ organizational training manuals
> ▸ customers or users
> ▸ annual reports
> ▸ expected audience members
> ▸ anything or anyone else you can think of.

Step 4: Write Your Presentation

This is when you take what you learned from steps 1–3, and put pencil to paper to coalesce the thoughts and ideas that you will present. Before you start to write, make sure once again that you are clear about your presentation's purpose. Do you want your audience to know something, be persuaded to do something, or to perform differently?

Because all presentations have a beginning, a middle, and a closing, let's follow that structure.

Opening. Your opening should do three things:

1. Grab your audience's attention.
2. Express the main point of your presentation.
3. Express the benefit or explain what the audience can expect to get out of the presentation.

As you begin to prepare your presentation, think about ways of grabbing your audience's attention. You can do this by focusing on the purpose of your presentation and expressing the benefit the audience will receive from hearing your presentation. Don't worry, though, if you can't think of a strong opening as you start to write your presentation. Some prefer to wait until they've written their presentation before trying to come up with a catchy opener.

Here is an example of an opening for a presentation the purpose of which is to inform trainers how to become more influential in adding value to their organizations: "Tonight I want to talk to you about the importance of making sure our training initiatives are valued and focused on helping to support the strategy of our organization."

If you're thinking that this doesn't sound at all exciting, you're right. Now compare it to this opening: "A major issue for trainers today is how to consistently demonstrate their value to those in the organizations they serve (main point).

Tonight you will learn a practical approach to do this that will enable you to use your power to influence the strategic direction of your organization" (benefit).

Which opening grabs your attention? The second example tells the audience not only the topic of the presentation, but expresses the benefit they will receive if they stay and listen. It also clearly and enthusiastically states the WIIFM for the audience, something that always gets people's attention.

The second example is written from the perspective of the audience members and emphasizes the value they would get out of the presentation, instead of the presenter. Compare "I want to talk about . . ." with "Tonight you will learn . . . ." The first phrase focuses on "I," the presenter, whereas the second focuses on "you," the audience. It's easy to see which is more effective.

Although not all openings for each presentation you do are going to sound the same, the opening you choose sets the stage for the presentation and often is the deciding factor as to whether your audience will be tuned in or not. If you grab them early, you'll keep them engaged. If you don't, it's awfully difficult to get them back.

Think About This

Don't underestimate the power of enthusiasm. In many ways it distinguishes great presenters from the good ones. Enthusiasm is infectious, and no amount of subject matter expertise can substitute for it.

Let's take a look at some other kinds of openers:

- ▶ *Jokes:* Some presenters like to lighten the mood by telling a joke. A joke can work if people find you funny and if you don't cross the line between good taste and bad. But, as most people know, not everyone is funny and can tell a joke. A general rule of thumb for jokes is if you have a question whether it would be appropriate to tell it then don't.

- ▶ *Humorous or relevant stories or anecdotes:* A story or anecdote can work well as an opening remark, but both require practice because few people are natural storytellers. There's more about stories and anecdotes later in this book.

- ▶ *An icebreaker or brief exercise:* An icebreaker is a short exercise that often serves as a means for audience members to introduce themselves and get to know each other. You can find more information in books and online about different kinds of icebreakers. An icebreaker can be an effective way of starting

Think About This

Think before you automatically incorporate an icebreaker into your presentation. You need to make sure it is going to work for the audience you are expecting. Some audiences tend to be more playful and open to expressing themselves, but others are more reserved and reluctant to do so. Use good judgment. Remember: If you start off with a dud, it's awfully difficult to recover.

your presentation provided that it's appropriate for the audience you are presenting to and you have enough time to do it.

▶ *A question:* You can ask either a rhetorical question ("How would you like to learn how to become more credible in order to influence your organization in achieving its strategic goals?"), or you can ask a real question ("How many people find they have at least a little influence in their organization?"). In the former you are not looking for a response, and in the latter you may simply call for a show of hands.

Basic Rule 6

Remember, audiences of all sizes need a reason to pay attention. Give them a good opening that will grab and hold their attention.

Middle. The middle of the presentation should specifically support the purpose and main point of the presentation and meet the needs of your audience based on your research. Normally, you will do this by using supporting points. These points support the purpose and main point. Because most people only remember a small part of the presentation, you'll want to limit the supporting points to a manageable number, somewhere between three and five of the most important ones.

The first thing you'll do is go back to the research that you've done about your audience's needs and the purpose of your presentation. Write down what you perceive to be the most important points that support in some way the presentation's purpose and main point. Write some notes that fully express each supporting point, but don't worry initially about how you are going to say it.

Next, review your notes and begin to pare down the supporting points to three to five strong ones. Once you have decided what they are, begin writing your notes. Do this in the way that seems to work best for you. Try writing two or three iterations each time, trimming down the wording so that eventually you get to the talking points you feel comfortable with. (Remember you don't want a script or anything lengthy.)

Some presenters prefer to use an outline format in which headings trigger your talking points for the presentation. Others want the comfort of having substantial notes to draw from. Beware when taking this approach because too many words are an invitation to read your notes verbatim. However, if you're going to err on one side, it probably makes more sense to have more information in your notes, at least initially in your career as a presenter, because copious notes can serve as a security blanket. And, it's also easier to take away information than add it.

In the example used earlier about a presentation on how trainers can become more influential in their organizations, the use of supporting points might look like the following: "A major issue for trainers today is how to consistently demonstrate their value to those in the organizations they serve (main point). Tonight you will learn a practical approach to do this so that you can use your power to influence the strategic direction of your organization (benefit). This requires you to establish your credibility by implementing the following three practices (supporting points):

1. knowing your business
2. acting strategically
3. understanding your organization's culture.

Think About This

If you give too much information in your presentation (maybe seven or eight supporting points instead of the three to five recommended here) because you think your audience *must* know it, you are only doing yourself and your audience a disservice by obscuring the really important issues, almost guaranteeing that the attendees won't remember much of anything you said. To get around this problem, you can opt to put much of the details in a handout people can take with them and read after the presentation.

"Let's take a look at each of the three, starting with the first—knowing your business . . ." (elaboration on each supporting point).

What you do then is elaborate on each of the supporting points making sure that what you say explains and supports the main point and purpose of the presentation.

Closing. The end of your presentation is usually what people remember most, so it is important to make your ending a memorable one. Some things to consider are:

▶ Do a quick review of all key points.
▶ Consider doing a quick review of the benefits the audience got from your presentation.
▶ If appropriate, you may ask for a call to action of some kind.
▶ Consider asking the audience if they have any questions.

Your ending should show enthusiasm, passion, and conviction. If not, you may find that the flatness of the ending is all your audience remembers of what otherwise was a very good presentation. Using the same example, a strong ending might be:

> "As you can see, trainers really do have a great deal more power to influence and add value to their organizations. I would challenge each of you to go back to your organization and make a conscious decision to focus your attention on establishing credibility by working to know your business better; acting more strategically with those you come in contact with; and searching to truly understand your organization's culture. If you do this you will be well on your way to adding value and making a difference in helping your organization achieve its goals."

Transitions. Transitions help you move from point to point in a smooth, flowing manner. They are segues to the different parts of your presentation and are important in making your presentation cohesive and understandable. Because people don't speak the way they write, try developing transitions using language you are comfortable with to connect the pieces of what you've written in your notes. For example, a transition based on the example used in this chapter might sound like this: "Another example of

Think About This

Good use of transitions makes your presentation flow smoothly from one point to the next. The more comfortable you are with the words you use, the more natural your presentation will sound.

establishing your credibility in your organization is understanding the business your business is in . . . ."

Step 5: Choose Your Audiovisuals

Because most people have an easier time remembering something they have seen, most presentations benefit from some use of audiovisual support. You need to decide which media will work best to support and enhance your presentation. These days many options are available to choose from. For example, in addition to the standard audiovisual tools—flipcharts, overhead transparencies, and video—you can generate "slides" with computer software such as Microsoft PowerPoint. Chapter 6 presents a more encompassing look at the kinds of audiovisuals that are available and which ones might work best for you.

Step 6: Practice, Practice, Practice

After all the analysis and preparation is completed and the important decisions are made, the final step before giving your presentation is to practice. The most effective way to practice depends to a great extent on the type of presentation you will be making and what you feel most comfortable with. For example, if you will be presenting without audiovisual support, an easy and effective practice method is to give the presentation over and over in front of someone you trust as if he or she were sitting in the audience.

If you add audiovisuals, then it is important that you incorporate them at some point into your practice routine so you become comfortable with using them. Don't underestimate the importance of gaining a comfort level with the audiovisuals you will be using. Although you may know your presentation and how to use your audiovisual aids, synchronizing them for your presentation takes practice.

Preparing for your presentations can take many forms. Practicing in front of a mirror or on videotape is especially helpful because you can see yourself as your audience will. Audiotaping yourself can be especially helpful because you will get a good idea of how you sound. If you have access to the room you are going to present in prior to your presentation, actually practicing in the room lends a certain sense of realism.

Although most people practice their presentation focusing on the verbal component, it's important to also concentrate on the nonverbal aspects. Don't forget to practice making eye contact, hand gestures, voice inflection, and your body language in general. As for the pitfall of overrehearsing, don't worry too much about it; you'll know when it's time to stop.

Getting It Done

Exercise 2-1 will allow you to not only revisit the major points in the chapter you just read, but you will also have the opportunity to hone your newly acquired skills and actually apply them to create your own presentation.

Exercise 2-1. Getting ready for your presentation.

1. I know the purpose of my presentation. Yes_____ No_____. Jot down some notes from discussions with your sponsor and others about your presentation's purpose:

   _____

   _____

2. I know my audience's needs. Yes_____ No_____. Jot down some notes here:

   _____

   _____

3. I understand my relationship to the audience. Yes_____ No_____. Jot down some notes here:

   _____

   _____

4. I have determined if the audience falls into the category of friends, strangers, or both. Yes_____ No_____. Jot down some notes here:

   _____

   _____

5. I have considered other important factors such as the following:
   - ☐ expertise and knowledge level of the audience
   - ☐ level of authority
   - ☐ who's in the audience:
     - ☐ peers
     - ☐ direct reports
     - ☐ decision makers
     - ☐ others_____

Jot down some notes here:

_____

_____

6. I am prepared to handle any anticipated
   ☐ skepticism   ☐ objections   ☐ indifference
   Jot down some notes here:

_____

_____

7. I know the size of the group I will be presenting to and am prepared to adjust my presentation accordingly. Yes_____ No_____. Jot down some notes here:

_____

_____

8. I have done the necessary research and know my subject. Yes_____ No_____. Jot down some notes here:

_____

_____

9. I am clear about how I wish to open my presentation. Yes_____ No_____. Jot down some notes here:

_____

_____

10. I am clear about the main point of my presentation. Yes_____ No_____. Jot down some notes here:

_____

_____

11. I know what supporting points I will use to support my main point. Yes_____ No_____. Jot down some notes here:

_____

_____

12. I know how I'll close my presentation. Yes_____ No_____. Jot down some notes here:

_____

_____

13. I have chosen the right audiovisuals for my presentation and know how to operate each.
Yes_____ No_____. Jot down some notes here:

_____

_____

14. I have practiced my presentation and feel confident and competent to deliver it.
Yes_____ No_____. Jot down some notes here:

_____

_____

In the next chapter you'll learn how all the time and effort taken preparing your presentation will reap dividends when you deliver an effective presentation that achieves your purpose and meets your audience's needs.

3

Getting Ready to Deliver Your Presentation

What's Inside This Chapter

Here, you'll see how to:
- ▶ Use the five basic truths for giving a presentation
- ▶ Deal with someone in your audience who knows more than you do about the subject matter
- ▶ Adapt your style to your audience's needs
- ▶ Use verbal skills to help get your message across
- ▶ Employ effective nonverbal skills to convey your message
- ▶ Relieve the anxiety that comes with making a presentation

After all the preparation comes the time to make your presentation. The freedom to enjoy this experience comes from knowing that you're prepared. So, go ahead and enjoy yourself! Have fun!

In the end people aren't going to remember where you held your hands or if you had a small lapse in memory. Your focus, instead, should be on achieving your purpose and meeting the needs of your audience. Even if you slip up, people are more apt to be forgiving if they believe you understood and respected their needs and that you did your very best. Don't put pressure on yourself to be the perfect presenter; it's going to take some time to get there. Remember that each time you present you'll get better and better.

The Five Basic Truths

Myriad publications by a host of respected presenters offer advice about delivering effective presentations. All this advice, though, can be distilled down to five basic truths about giving presentations:

▶ *Truth Number 1: There is no one way to make a presentation.* Think of the elements of your presentation on a continuum. On one end are things you should definitely be doing. On the other end are things you probably should not do. It's the middle where the freedom lies to pick and choose what you believe will work best for you and your audience. In this book you'll have a look at what works, what doesn't, and ways to make wise choices about all the things between.

▶ *Truth Number 2: You know more than your audience.* In most instances this is true. There may be instances when someone in your audience knows as much—or even more—about your subject than you do. Rather than feel threatened, seasoned presenters take advantage of this situation by recognizing the great wealth of knowledge and experience that exists in the room and by using other experts as allies to support what they are presenting.

Think About This

Feeling threatened by so-called experts in your audience can have a detrimental effect on your performance. And, looking threatened is even worse. Although it's easy to feel intimidated, you'll gain more credibility with your audience when you show enough confidence to allow other experts in your audience to express their thoughts and opinions about a subject.

▶ *Truth Number 3: There are "need to knows," and there are "nice to knows."* Good presenters focus on need-to-know information and understand that because the audience can only absorb so much information, it should be that which offers the most benefit.

▶ *Truth Number 4: Making a presentation is not a science; it's an art.* With any form of art there are different ways an artist can interpret his or her subject, all of which may be valid. What's most important is that the interpretation makes a connection with those experiencing it. It's the same thing with a presentation. Two presenters can approach a topic in different ways and still achieve their purpose and meet their audiences' needs. So, treat your presentation as your art and a way of expressing yourself and leave science in the lab.

▶ *Truth 5: The best presentations are those you are passionate about.* Having a passion for what you do is the best elixir for any butterflies you might have as you stand before your audience. Passion is expressed in many ways, from the exuberance on your face, to the skip in your step, to the conviction in your voice. Passionate presentations help create passionate learners.

Style and Technique

Although there are many different ways to present, there are certain methods and skills that seem to work best in most situations. These tend to fall into two categories: style and technique.

Style

Some presenters pride themselves on having a certain style that they use while making a presentation. Having a style works great if making presentations is your business. Most of you who are reading this book, though, will probably use a combination of different styles that you're comfortable with and that your audiences seem to respond to. You'll do this because of the wide range of audiences you'll present to, all with varying needs and responding to different styles.

For example, when an audience comes to a program given by a world-class consultant like Tom Peters, author of the best-selling book *In Search of Excellence: Lessons From America's Best-Run Companies* (Warner Books, 1988), it expects a presenter whose style is exciting and full of energy, someone with strong opinions. The audiences you'll be presenting to, in general, are probably less interested in your style as long as you cover the subject competently, keep their interest, and are respectful of their needs. Of course, it helps that you aren't charging them a $50,000 fee to hear you speak!

Noted

Watch those who are in the public eye or others who inspire you and compel you to listen. See what they do that separates them from the rest.

Think About This

One size does not fit all. This adage is especially true of presentations. For example, you may choose to be more facilitative in a workshop as you involve your audience in the learning, but you may be more inclined to showcase your expertise at a presentation where people have come to hear you speak on a topic.

Still, presenters tend to gravitate toward one or two styles that they are comfortable with, although even their choice of styles tends to be situational. As you make more presentations you will find that your style will often reflect a combination of factors including your personality, the culture of the organization you are representing or presenting to, the subject matter, the kind of presentation you are making, and other related factors.

Try not to get too hung up on a style, especially early in your presenting career. Your style can be developed as you do more and more presentations. Nevertheless, any style you adopt needs to meet two criteria:

1. Your style needs to reflect who you are as a person and professional, meaning that you're always prepared and that you demonstrate a level of confidence that tells your audience that you know what you're talking about. Audiences are able to see through any attempt to cover a lack of preparedness and confidence with a slick style.

2. Your audience needs to respond positively to your style. It's one thing for you to feel at ease while presenting to your audience, but you need to gauge how your audience responds to you and your style. The presentations you make are for your audience's sake, not just yours. As you get more practice, begin to pay closer attention to how audiences respond to you, and don't hesitate to try some things that are new or different.

As you begin to develop your style, try to remember a few simple rules:

1. Whatever style you choose, be passionate about your subject. This admonition applies even for subjects you are less than excited about. Remember that low excitement from you means low reaction from your audience.

2. A presentation style is a means to an end, so don't make the focus of your presentation you; instead make it the subject you are presenting.

3. Style without substance should never be an alternative unless your goal is purely to entertain. Start with your purpose in mind, and let it be your guide.

4. Use a style of presentation that reflects the needs of your audience. Each audience is unique. Recognize that the group of engineers you are about to present to may respond with less enthusiasm to a call for audience participation than the HR professionals you presented to last week.

5. Don't get stuck in one presentation style. Try changing things up every now and then. This advice is especially true if most of your presentations are to the same audiences. It's easy to fall into a predictable pattern as a presenter, a tendency that audiences soon tire of.

6. Let the subject matter influence the style you use. If the subject is a serious one, then treat it that way. Conversely, a light-hearted approach may be the best way to treat less-serious subjects. Use your judgment: For example, starting a presentation on sexual harassment in the workplace with a joke might not be good idea.

Think About This

Some easy ways to get feedback from your audience is to ask for it. After your presentation, consider doing an informal evaluation by asking audience members specific questions about what they thought of the presentation and whether it met their needs. Some presentations automatically include a formal written evaluation. Most tend to be "smile" sheets, so if you are seeking specific information, either develop your own evaluation or ask the sponsor if you can include some specific questions in the evaluation. Use this feedback to help improve your presentation skills.

Basic Rule 7

Don't worry about developing a style; it will come. Focus more on achieving your purpose and meeting the audience's needs, and you'll do fine.

Think About This

Try personalizing your message as a way of showing commitment to what you are saying by using "I" and "me" when making your points. Certainly this might not be appropriate for every presentation but many times it is, especially when you are trying to persuade someone to your way of thinking or to take some action. People are more apt to listen to someone who seems to care about what he or she is saying than someone who doesn't.

Technique

Understand that the message of your presentation passes through you to your audience and that you have control over how it is transmitted. Certain methods and techniques work better than others for ensuring that your message is delivered clearly and coherently, but also that it captures your audience's attention. Think of it this way: If your audience doesn't get the message, you can throw everything else out the window.

Presentation skills fall into two basic categories: verbal and nonverbal. In some ways speaking to an audience is pretty much the same as speaking with someone one-on-one. For example, both require that the speaker be clear and articulate in order for the person or persons to understand the message being sent. But, important distinctions exist.

Verbal Skills

Certain verbal skills, however, come into play when presenting to a group. Take the size of the room you're in, for example. It's much easier for someone to ask you for clarification when he or she is one-on-one with you than when you are presenting to a group in a large room. It's also easier to determine when someone doesn't understand something you've said when dealing one-on-one than when you are speaking to a group. The following sections cover some basic verbal skills to focus on when you are making a presentation to a group.

Voice Projection. Your audience has to be able to hear you in every part of the room when you present. Here's a simple way to make sure you are projecting adequately: Before your presentation have someone stand in the furthest reaches of the room, begin your presentation, and ask if he or she can hear you. Then simply adjust your projection as necessary. Remember, though, it's easier for one person in the back of the room to hear you during a practice session than it is for an entire audience to hear you because of the normal din in the room. So, be sure to ratchet your voice projection up a little bit from your rehearsal voice.

Pitch. The dreaded monotone voice has been the bane of many a presenter. Everyone has listened to presenters who drone on for 45 minutes and never modulate their pitch up or down. This usually happens when a presenter relies too heavily on his or her written notes, paying more attention to saying all the words and less to how the words sound. Try varying the pitch of your voice in relation to what you are saying.

Noted

Try to never start off a presentation by asking the audience, "Can you hear me all right?" Take care of that issue before you take the podium.

For example, when you are saying something that you are excited about, let it come across in your voice. If you follow with something more serious, modulate your pitch to accentuate the change in feeling. Your audience will take its cues not only from what you say but, sometimes even more important, how you say it.

Filler Words. Almost everyone, at some point, uses what are called filler words or sounds. Typical ones are "uh," "okay," "um," "you know," and "like." These words and sounds are used to fill in silences as people search for words. They tend to be habits and are often used when the presenter is anxious during the presentation. From a presenter's standpoint, the problem with these filler words is that they become so obvious that the audience pays more attention to them than the point of the presentation.

The best way of dealing with filler words is to be prepared—pure and simple. Another way is to become aware of what filler words you use and, while you practice, make a conscious

Think About This

Don't get bogged down trying to be too perfect in how you say things during your presentation. What's most important is that the words you say come naturally and with feeling.

effort to not say them. Still another way is to insert intentional pauses in your presentation. Sometimes this slows things down just enough to help you eliminate some of the fillers. The more aware you are of their usage, the easier it is to eliminate them. What you don't want to do is to become so obsessed about using filler words that you upset the flow of your presentation.

Pronunciation. If your audience can't understand what you are saying, it's as if you didn't say it, so make sure you pronounce your words in a way that your audience will understand. Certain parts of the country use slightly different dialects that might be a bit strange in other areas. Check with the locals beforehand to ensure that your message will be heard as it was intended.

Rate. Good presenters can adjust their rate of speaking to accentuate a feeling or mood. Although the average rate of speech is about 140 words per minute, to show enthusiasm or energy for a particular point try increasing the amount of words accordingly. To make an important point perfectly clear or to emphasize something, try slowing down the rate to as low as 100 words per minute. This isn't science, so you don't have to get out the stopwatch and count your words. Rather, understand that you can create a mood and atmosphere for your presentation just by how you use your voice.

Basic Rule 8
You are responsible for ensuring that the message passes through you to your audience. Take this responsibility seriously.

Nonverbal Skills
Based on different studies, it is usually accepted that between 7 to 10 percent of the effectiveness of a presentation comes from the words the presenter uses. Therefore, at least 90 percent of the effectiveness must come from nonverbal messages sent by the presenter, rather a strange phenomenon considering that most of the presenting you'll do will be by way of words. The fact remains, though, that people tend to remember what they see more than what they hear.

The effect of nonverbal messages depends in large part on the kind of presentation you are making, who your audience is, what your relationship is to it, and a whole host of factors that determine the significance of your nonverbal behavior. As a presenter it's important to recognize that it's not only about the words, but it's also about how the words are presented. The following sections describe some nonverbal skills that are worth paying attention to while making a presentation.

Stance. Being comfortable and natural while making your presentation is important. However, you want to avoid appearing overly casual with your audience. Something as simple as how you stand before your audience indicates to them the level of importance you are placing on what you have to say.

A general rule of thumb is to stand with legs apart around 18 inches or so (depending on your size), have an equal distribution of weight on each foot, and with your arms in a comfortable position. Once again, presenting is not science, so taking into consideration your style and the factors already mentioned, adjust these recommendations as needed.

Here are some simple guidelines to follow:

- Take your hands out of your pockets.
- Don't slouch.
- Don't rock back and forth on your heels.
- Don't tap your feet.
- Don't drum your fingers on a desk, table, or lectern.

Think About This

Some presenters look perfectly natural and professional leaning against a desk, but some who seem to follow all the rules come off as less then credible. Maybe it's because they try too hard or simply that other aspects of their style are out of sync. Less-experienced presenters sometimes try to follow "the rules" to the letter and end up looking like robots. Don't over-analyze your presentation. You've got enough to think about.

You've probably guessed by now that all of these guidelines fall under the categories of awareness and common sense. Don't worry if you slip up occasionally—it's not the end of the world! None of them is a total presentation destroyer. Be yourself, do your best, and learn from any mistakes you make.

Think About This

Be aware of your habits that might be distracting when you are standing in front of your audience. Use good judgment in deciding how you wish to be perceived. The goal is not to be perfect; it's to do what you can to establish an environment that helps meet your audience's needs.

Body Movement. Many new presenters ask, "Should I be moving or standing still when I make a presentation?" Here's the answer: It depends! Body movement, as it relates to giving a presentation, means any physical repositioning for a purpose such as walking to another spot or a casual pace. Certainly hand and body gestures are a part of movement, but they are discussed separately.

It's important to consider what messages you send as you make body movements while presenting. In general, use movement when you want to convey enthusiasm and energy about a particular point in your presentation. Some seasoned presenters walk to another part of the room while speaking, all the while maintaining eye contact with the audience. Others move at a slow pace, maintaining eye contact and almost mesmerizing their audience who listens carefully to each word they say. Movement, in both cases, is meant to convey to the audience the importance of a point the presenter feels strongly about and that the audience should pay attention to.

You can also use movement to engage all the members of the audience, especially when addressing a large audience. A good way to do this is to move toward different parts of the room as you speak, making personal contact with different pockets of people in the room. This technique keeps those sitting on the side, for example, as engaged as those directly in front of you.

Noted

A word of caution: Remember, there's a fine line between movement that is purposeful and movement that is distracting.

Movement can also be used to emphasize a point. When addressing a small audience, try approaching an audience member by walking toward him or her and briefly speaking directly to the person. Then, continue by refocusing your attention on the entire audience. This technique is a dramatic way of stressing a point, although it may take some time and practice to master. It's worth trying when you are more comfortable in your presenter role.

Movement is an important part of using audiovisuals, too. There is a tendency when using such visuals as overhead transparencies or a flipchart and easel for the presenter to stand anchored where the equipment has been placed. When this happens, it's easy for the audience to start anticipating the next overhead to go up on the screen instead of listening to what the presenter is saying. To prevent the focus from becoming the visuals, try moving away now and then from the visual. This technique helps the audience to maintain a focus on you and your presentation.

Movement can be used to draw attention to something going on in a certain part of the room. For example, when someone is answering a question and his or her attention is directed toward the presenter, the presenter can move toward the audience member and, with a gentle sweep of the hand, gesture to the audience, encouraging the speaker to direct their remarks to the entire group, not just the presenter. This technique is a powerful tool to use during presentations in which group interaction is an important ingredient for success.

Movement helps maintain the audience's interest. By moving in a purposeful way during the presentation, the presenter helps people maintain interest and keeps the presentation flowing along. In fact, this technique not only keeps the audience engaged in what is being presented, but also helps the presenter stay involved.

Think About This

In some instances during your presentation it's wise to show little or no movement. This advice holds true especially in situations where you want the audience to focus attention on a specific part of your message and you don't want any chance that it will be distracted by your moving around. Although some planning of movement is helpful, movement that looks overly rehearsed comes off as stilted and detracts from the presentation. The key, once again, is to be natural and purposeful with what works best for you.

Gestures. Gestures refer to hand and body movements and are an important part of any presentation. When you watch a play, the actors use gestures to convey emotions, add emphasis to particular points, and paint a mental picture of what the scene is about. Giving a presentation is very similar to acting on stage, especially in light of the fact that about 90 percent of your message is expressed through nonverbal messages. Here are some tips about gestures:

▶ Make sure gestures are purposeful and within the context of what you are presenting.

▶ Too many hand gestures can be a distraction to your audience, so know when enough is enough.

▶ Use gestures for emphasis. For example, if you say, "There are five steps in the coaching process," try using your fingers to visually count out one, two, three, four, and five.

▶ When calling on someone in the audience, try casually extending your arm toward that person and with a gentle sway acknowledge him or her.

▶ Watch the fidgeting, playing with your magic marker, cracking your knuckles—all these gestures are very distracting.

▶ Do your best to recognize and eliminate any distracting or annoying habits, such as playing with your ear, hair, jewelry, mustache, or glasses.

▶ Remove any loose change, keys, or other objects from your pockets before a presentation so you don't get caught jingling them.

▶ When calling on someone in the audience, never point at him or her, because this gesture can easily be misconstrued as a sign of disrespect.

Eye Contact. Everyone knows the value of maintaining good eye contact when making a presentation. Making eye contact is important for a number of reasons. First, it is a sign of respect to audience members, and it shows that you are engaged with them, demonstrating that your presentation is truly audience-centered. For example, your perspective changes when you think of your audience as 15 individuals as opposed to one big group. Next, similar to a one-on-one conversation, no one seems especially trustworthy if he or she doesn't look the other person in the eye. This concept also applies for a presentation, only now it's a number of different people.

But, how much eye contact is enough? As a general rule of thumb spend five or six seconds of eye contact at least once with each member of your audience, making sure that you look at everyone when presenting to a small group and to small pockets of people in a larger audience. Eye contact is also an opportunity for a presenter to get a feel for how his or her audience is reacting to the presentation. By making eye contact and seeing people's expressions, the presenter can often tell whether the audience is showing interest, following what is being presented, and is being engaged in the presentation.

Facial Expression. Facial expressions convey emotion and are often the passageway to what a presenter is truly feeling about the points he or she is making. When presenters realize the power their expressions have they understand that they can change the mood of the room simply by changing the look on their face.

One of the easiest actions to take while presenting is smiling. In addition, a smile can pay dividends, too. Smiles are often interpreted by your audience as a sign of a presenter's confidence, as well as his or her comfort and commitment to the subject. Although some people find it difficult to smile and talk at the same time, it's something well worth practicing.

Think About This

Here's a suggestion for making eye contact. It's called "Make a Friend." Find someone in the room who seems particularly interested in your presentation. Maybe it's the big smile on his or her face, or maybe it's someone who has heard you before and liked what he or she heard. This person is now your "friend" in the room. Start by making your initial eye contact with your friend. As you continue making eye contact with the other audience members, always come back to your friend in the room to keep your momentum. This person serves as a focal point and his or her positive reaction can give you a boost whenever you need one.

Basic Rule 9
People trust what they see more than what they hear.

Other Points to Remember
In addition to style and technique, there are a couple other methods and skills you'll want to develop.

The First 90 Seconds
The first 90 seconds of a presentation are the most important because that's when the tone is set for the rest of the presentation. If you start off on the right foot,

Think About This

Self-talk can be a powerful tool for getting prepared for any challenge, especially one like giving a presentation. It's helpful to differentiate between negative self-talk and positive self-talk. Compare "I'll never be able to get up before that group and explain to them the new benefits package . . ." with "I know what I'm talking about, and I can give this presentation so that the others will understand this new benefits package too." Imagine how you would feel saying each of these two statements to yourself. Using positive self-talk (and being prepared, of course) increases your chances of accomplishing your goal by quantum leaps.

chances are you'll continue along that path. If, however, you start off on the wrong foot, it can be very difficult to recover. That's why great presenters have the first 90 seconds of their presentation down pat. Once again, it's all about being prepared. When you start strong your audience becomes energized and its interest is piqued.

Some experienced presenters start with an interesting or humorous story, slowly building to the essence of their presentation. Others hit hard with a benefit statement that makes it very clear why the audience should listen to the presentation. Find your own way of starting, practice it until you know it, and then do it. As you gain experience, you'll become more confident about adding to your repertoire of strong openings.

Once you know what you are going to say, consider some of these suggestions for that first 90 seconds:

- ▸ Look like you're confident even if your knees are shaking.
- ▸ Acknowledge your audience, smile (if appropriate), and start talking.
- ▸ Exhibit an outward appearance that says to your audience that there isn't any other place you'd rather be.

Basic Rule 10

Have the first 90 seconds of your presentation down cold. Starting strong builds momentum to help carry you through your presentation.

- Begin by painting a mental picture with your words and actions for the audience right from the start.
- Be focused, positive, enthusiastic, and speak confidently.

Overcoming Nervousness

First, it's normal to be nervous. In fact, if you aren't at least a little nervous, you need to seriously question whether you are ready to give a presentation, because nerves can give you the "edge" that often gets the adrenaline going.

Noted

Nervous energy can work for you. If you've ever played a sport or acted in a play, for example, you will know that a little nervousness before you start gets the adrenaline flowing and can actually enhance your performance. Of course, too much of anything can turn a positive into a negative. The same goes for nervous energy too, so know yourself and just how much you need to get you going.

To deal with nervousness before your presentation consider taking the following measures:

- Try to arrive at least 15 to 30 minutes before your presentation to get comfortable in the room and deal with any potential issues that can affect your presentation and increase your anxiety.
- Have a preparation routine that includes checking all audiovisual equipment; room setup and other logistics; additional instructions from your sponsor about issues of time, revised audience numbers, ways to handle late arrivals, and so forth; getting a glass of water ready; and anything else that will alleviate possible pitfalls.
- If appropriate, verify with your sponsor your starting time, how you will be introduced, and your ending time.
- Use positive self-talk as a way of convincing yourself that you'll be fine.
- Drink some water to get rid of dry mouth, but watch your

Think About This

Know how you are going to deal with late arrivals before your presentation. Don't unduly penalize those who arrive on time by waiting for those who are late.

caffeine intake because it can make people a little hyperactive or shaky.

▶ Use a visioning technique before your presentation where you play a "tape" of the first 90 seconds in your head.

▶ Confront your fear by reminding yourself that most people have a fear of giving a presentation so what you are experiencing is quite natural.

▶ Take a series of deep breaths and exhale slowly.

▶ Keep your presentation in perspective; this isn't life and death!

You've noticed that the emphasis has been on being prepared—both mentally and physically. If you still aren't sure you know how to operate your PowerPoint presentation, all the deep breathing in the world is not going to help you much. *Be prepared,* and you'll be fine.

Getting It Done

Complete the checklist in exercise 3-1 before delivering your presentation.

Exercise 3-1. Delivering your presentation.

1. I'm fully prepared and ready to give my presentation. Yes_____ No_____. Jot down some notes here:

   _____

   _____

   _____

2. I'm prepared to adapt my style to meet what I perceive the needs of my audience to be. Yes_____ No_____. Jot down some notes here:

   _____

   _____

   _____

3. I've practiced the skills and techniques I will use to give my presentation. Yes_____ No_____. Jot down some notes here:

   _____

   _____

   _____

4. I have a clear vision of what my presentation will look like when I present it.
   Yes_____ No_____. Jot down some notes here:

   _____

   _____

   _____

5. I have a positive attitude about my presentation, and I'm ready to go. Yes_____ No_____.
   Jot down some notes here:

   _____

   _____

   _____

In the next chapter, you'll learn about the skills you can develop to make the leap from presenter to facilitator.

4

The Art of Facilitation

■ ■

What's Inside This Chapter

Here, you'll see how to:

▶ Develop your role as a facilitator
▶ Incorporate facilitation skills into your presentation
▶ Determine whether to ask questions
▶ Ask the right kinds of questions to get your audience to participate
▶ Conduct a question-and-answer session
▶ Make the transition from one subject to another
▶ Use the most effective facilitation techniques to enhance your presentation
▶ Decide when and how to use humor in your presentation

If you've ever participated in any group workshop experience, you are probably familiar with the term facilitation. Sometimes presenters speak about "facilitating a group discussion" or just simply "facilitating a group." Facilitation, like much of what you've learned so far, is much more an art than a science. Like artists who must learn the basic elements of their art before they can paint or compose, so, too, a facilitator must also understand the basic elements of facilitation to use it effectively in a presentation.

What Is Facilitation?

Facilitation is a technique used by a presenter to involve his or her audience and help members of a group or audience learn from one another through the open sharing of thoughts, opinions, and ideas. In the role of facilitator, the presenter uses such techniques as questioning, silence, paraphrasing, and various nonverbal cues to encourage the audience to participate in the experience and learning. Although not every presentation you make will require facilitation skills, it's important to be prepared to act as a facilitator when the time comes.

Think About This

Most presenters are involved at one point or another in conducting question-and-answer, or Q & A, sessions as part of their presentation. To keep the discussion moving, presenters often rely on facilitation skills to involve the audience. Learning to use these skills effectively, however, takes practice because good facilitation requires the facilitator to be able to anticipate situations and not just respond to them.

Becoming an effective facilitator requires practice, although good facilitators possess a certain intuition. They know, for example, when to ask a question and when to be silent; when to challenge a statement and when to remain neutral. Although you can't teach someone to be intuitive, you can learn the basics of facilitation and practice them as you make presentations, as well as in your everyday interactions with others.

Think of a presentation you've attended, when the presenter was able to create an atmosphere where people in the audience learned as much from one another as they did from the presenter. In all probability the "facilitator" asked good, challenging questions, listened more than spoke, and served as more of a guide than as an instructor. The facilitator probably answered questions in a way that was clear, respectful, and consistent with the subject being presented.

Here are some quick tips to help you develop your role as a facilitator. Effective facilitators are able to

▶ create an open environment by encouraging people to participate in the learning, and maintaining people's self-esteem

- ▶ set guidelines for audience participation, by respecting others' thoughts and ideas, ensuring there are no unnecessary interruptions, and staying on point
- ▶ acknowledge people who participate by praising and thanking them for their contributions and encouraging them to continue to participate
- ▶ create transitions between questions asked and answered by audience members, as well as between topic areas ("That answer was right on target. Does anyone else have a thought?" "Thank you, Jean, for your question. This leads us to a second issue I'd like to raise . . .")
- ▶ be honest with what they know and don't know; acknowledging what is opinion and what is fact
- ▶ express an opinion when appropriate but makes sure that audience members' feelings and opinions are not being judged as invalid or wrong
- ▶ give everyone an opportunity to participate but never forcing anyone who chooses not to
- ▶ keep the discussion flowing and on target while recognizing when to end a discussion and move on.

The techniques involved in being an effective facilitator are ones that must be practiced many times to become proficient. When facilitating, it's just as important to know when to use certain techniques as how to use them. Even seasoned facilitators learn something new each time they do a presentation, because every one offers different challenges. This chapter focuses on some of the more useful techniques, especially relating to the new or inexperienced presenter.

Basic Rule 11

Remember that there is no quick path to becoming a good facilitator. It's an art that must be practiced over and over.

Asking Questions

Not every presentation you make includes asking your audience questions. However, the more presentations you do, the greater the likelihood that asking questions will become an integral part of how you present. To ask good questions requires some thought because there are different kinds of questions for different purposes. Most people are aware of the two basic forms of questions: open-ended and closed-ended. There is, however, a third option—the hypothetical question—that's worth considering.

Noted

Be careful when asking the audience to join in to answer a question from an audience member. Although it's a good way to get the audience involved, it is also a good way to lose control of your audience.

Open-Ended Questions

Open-ended questions are those that generally call for more than a one-word answer. Open-ended questions enable the audience members to express their thoughts, ideas, feelings, and opinions.

For example, you might ask an open-ended question if you were speaking to an audience of co-workers gathered to hear you address their concerns regarding the company's new computerized time-tracking system. You might start with: "How has our new computerized time tracking system affected your work?" This kind of question affords the audience members an opportunity to express their feelings and opinions about the system, as well as what their experience has been up to this point.

Asking an open-ended question is an excellent way of getting your audience involved in the learning, and it generates group synergy. Open-ended questions often start with

- ▶ "Tell me about . . ."
- ▶ "Why . . . ?"
- ▶ "What do you think about . . . ?"
- ▶ "How . . . ?"

Usually questions that start this way help audience members to expound upon their answers, revealing information that can be helpful in the discussion.

Closed-Ended Questions

Closed-ended questions are sometimes preferable to open-ended ones in certain situations. Closed-ended questions are excellent for getting at specific facts and information.

For example, if you want to know whether a member of the audience had read the material you had sent out prior to your presentation, you would ask a closed-ended question to allow him or her to answer the question with a yes or no: "Did you have a chance to read the materials I sent out last week?" In fact, in this situation, chances are you aren't interested in an explanation from the audience member, only whether the person read the material.

Closed-ended questions often begin with

- ▶ "Who . . . ?"
- ▶ "Where . . . ?"
- ▶ "When . . . ?"
- ▶ "Did you . . . ?"

Hypothetical Questions

Hypothetical questions are great at getting people to think freely in situations where many answers may be valid. They often start with "What if . . . ?" Here's an example of a hypothetical question posed to a group of customer service representatives during a presen-

Noted

Be prepared to ask different kinds of questions before your presentation. Start by knowing why you are asking a question, and then ask the most appropriate question for your purpose.

tation on handling difficult customers: "What if a customer that you were speaking with on the phone got so angry that he or she threatened to take their business to a competitor? How would you handle it?"

Hypothetical questions are excellent discussion starters because they allow the audience to take an issue, problem, or situation and argue different ways of handling it. Because they are so good at inspiring people to join in, it's important that when posing a hypothetical question you are aware of any time constraints you have. It's very easy to lose track of time when the discussion gets lively.

Basic Rule 12

Don't waste your questions. Before you ask, know what it is you want to know.

Q & A Sessions

For many presentations, you or your sponsor may decide to have a Q & A session as part of the presentation. Questions and answers are generated by both you and your audience and, in some cases, by audience members asking each other questions about a particular subject. In fact, many experienced presenters evaluate the effectiveness of their presentation by the kinds of questions sparked by it.

Think About This

The prospect of food has a tendency to alter the minds of those in the audience about whether to ask questions. No one wants to miss the coffee and donuts! If you are really sincere about having people raise questions, refrain from saying, "Well, I guess I'm the only thing standing between you and lunch, but does anyone have any questions?" Exactly what do you think they are going to do?

You may choose to ask your audience questions either during the presentation or at its conclusion. Tell your audience at the beginning of your presentation when you plan to entertain questions, but never ask for questions right before a break or other times right before food is to be served.

Deciding whether to have a Q & A session and whether it should be during or at the end of the presentation are decisions you can make based on the nature of your subject and the kind of presentation you are making. To help you decide, ask yourself three questions:

1. *What is the purpose of my presentation?* If your presentation topic is a "need to know" and not just a "nice to know," try your best to work in at least some time for questions.

2. *How much time do I have to deliver the presentation?* You may wish to play it safe and save the questions to a period after your presentation because you'll know exactly how much time is remaining for your Q & A session. You can set it up in the beginning by saying, "After my presentation we'll have a little time for questions."

3. *How large is the group?* A large, eager group plus limited time often leads to many questions. If you are going to start a Q & A session, set a time when you will stop, and stick to it.

Noted

If you have more material to present than time to present it, it's okay to explain time constraints to your audience and offer to answer questions at the end of your presentation if time is available.

Here are some pointers to remember as you conduct a Q & A session:

▶ Think before asking your question, knowing what your goal is and what information you seek.

- Ask the question first and then allow the audience enough time (at least six to eight seconds) to respond.
- Do a quick check for understanding. If you get confused looks, try rephrasing the question.
- Be careful not to single out one person to answer the question before you ask it.
- Wait for hands to go up, and choose someone whom you think knows the answer.
- Don't call on the same people over and over or you'll run the risk of discouraging the rest of the group from asking questions of their own.
- When calling on people to answer questions, address them by their first names whenever possible.
- If someone's answer is clearly off base or seems to indicate that he or she didn't quite understand the question, very gently let the person off the hook by asking it again in a slightly different way. For example: "That's one way of looking at it, but actually what I was asking about was . . . ."
- Thank the person for answering the question and move on.

Think About This

Always allow audience members enough time to respond to your questions. Insufficient time is a clear message to your audience members that you really don't value their participation.

Follow these guidelines when answering a question from your audience:

- Anticipate the questions you might be asked, and prepare suitable responses before your presentation.
- Before answering, make sure you understand the question. If not, ask for clarification.
- Consider repeating the question for large audiences and rooms so that everyone can hear it. A word of caution here: Doing this for every question can be tedious, so, if possible, arrange

Think About This

Never call on anyone who doesn't seem to know the answer or who appears not to want to be called upon. This could be embarrassing to the individual and could ruin your credibility with the group.

Think About This

Calling audience members by name helps put the rest of the audience at ease. Even if you don't know the person's name, consider asking for it before you respond and then using the person's name as part of your response. In addition to being a professional and polite thing to do, it also helps you build your credibility with the group.

for a wireless microphone that can be passed to each questioner.

▶ Before answering a question, pause and think through your answer.

▶ If you don't know the answer, tell the questioner (and, if appropriate, the entire audience) that you will get the answer as soon as you are able to.

▶ Keep answers brief and to the point, being careful about rattling off statistics, large amounts of data, or confusing information.

▶ After answering a question, check the audience's body language and facial expression to see if your answer is clear. Clarify, if necessary, thank the person for the question, and move on.

Transitions

Effective presenters use transitions to segue between questions and answers on the same topic, as well as between topics. Transitions are important because they help the

Think About This

Never do anything that might embarrass an audience member, even though his or her question may seem to be coming from Mars. Even a joking reference to an audience member whose question may seem off the mark, can be taken by other audience members as a show of disrespect and lessen your credibility with the group.

discussion flow smoothly and make it easier for the audience to participate. The following are some examples of how transitions can be used:

▶ "Thank you, Lisa. That was an excellent question. Does anyone else have a question?"

▶ "That's my take on it. Does anyone have a different point of view?"

▶ "Let's move on to another subject. What do you think about . . . ?"

Silence

In our society even short periods of silence have a way of making people uncomfortable. Nevertheless, silence can be an excellent facilitation tool because it creates just enough tension to get people thinking. When you ask a question, give people some time to think their ideas through and formulate a response. If audience members don't respond, don't automatically let them off the hook. Try rephrasing the question or asking a follow-up question along the same lines as the first.

For example, you could ask an open-ended question, such as: "How has our new computer tracking system affected your work?" After about six to eight seconds of silence (or whatever seems appropriate for your particular presentation), you could try: "Okay, how about if we narrow it down a bit and start with how it has made it easier for you to do your work. Who'd like to start?"

Noted

Be careful about what you promise your audience. If you are unable to answer a question but can get the answer either during or after the presentation, explain this to your audience and follow through. If you can get the answer to the audience members but not before they leave, you'll need a way to get in touch with them afterward. Depending on the size of the group, you may decide to ask for their business cards, email addresses, or phone numbers to do this.

Active Listening

Effective facilitators are also good listeners. Active listening is especially useful during Q & A sessions. It requires concentration because you are not only listening to the verbal message, but also paying attention to the underlying emotion expressed by the person who is speaking. This part of the message is often reflected in the tone of the person's voice or inflection, as well as in nonverbal messages, such as facial expression and gestures. This underlying message usually

Think About This

When answering a question that has some relevance for the entire group, start by establishing eye contact with the person asking the question, then continue by responding to and making eye contact with the rest of the audience. Remember, unless the answer to a question is only specific to the questioner, think of questions as opportunities to provide information to the entire group, not just one person.

Basic Rule 13

Being an effective facilitator is often less about what you say and more about what you don't say. Sometimes silence creates just enough tension to get the discussion moving.

reflects the true meaning of what is being expressed. An example is the audience member, with a confused expression on her face, saying, "Sure, I think I understand what you are talking about." In this situation, the look of confusion indicates she clearly doesn't.

Noted

Want some pointers on how to work your audience? Watch how comedians work a room with devices as simple as a look or timed pause to allow the audience to "catch up" to the joke. You can pick up many good presenting tips from these professional presenters.

Paraphrasing is a form of active listening. Good facilitators are skillful at feeding back, in their own words, what an audience member has stated in order to further the understanding for themselves, as well as the rest of the audience.

Going back to the example of the presentation on the time-tracker system and the question asked about how the audience felt about it, an audience member might respond: "It's all right, I guess, but many of us feel that it slows down our work to the point where we can't get our real work done."

The presenter may paraphrase and say, "You sound frustrated because the system seems to be working against you, instead of for you," to which the audience member might respond, "Yeah, that's exactly what I mean."

By paraphrasing the audience member's statement and focusing on gaining clarity around both the meaning and feeling, the presenter was able to sum up for the audience the sense of frustration at least one audience member felt, as well as the fact that the system had the opposite effect for some than it was intended to do.

A seasoned facilitator then might use this information to probe further, following up thus: "Does anyone feel the same way about the system as Jean?"

Nonverbal Cues

Facilitators use nonverbal cues to encourage audience members to speak or to show approval—or disapproval—of a behavior. For example, a smile, sometimes with an extended arm and open palm facing upward (never a pointing finger), is often interpreted by an audience member as an invitation to say something or respond to a question.

Gently nodding your head "yes" (with a smile) is a sign of acknowledgement to an audience member and says in effect, "good answer" or "keep going." Locking eyes on an audience member who's displaying distracting behavior can serve as a gentle, respectful reminder that his or her behavior is inappropriate and should stop.

Think About This

A subtle form of active listening is "listening" with your eyes. You do this by observing your audience's nonverbal reactions as you speak. For example, smiling faces, nodding heads, and laughter are usually good indications that the audience is with you. No movement, no smiles, or disinterested looks usually indicate a need to adjust your presentation, pick up the energy, or maybe even to check with your audience to determine if they are getting the message you are sending.

Don't underestimate the power of these cues. Practice them, remembering that sometimes it's not what you say but what you *don't say* that has meaning for your audience. For a really good way to analyze and practice your nonverbal behavior, try videotaping yourself. It's a real eye-opener!

Rhetorical Questions

Rhetorical questions are really not questions at all because they are used not to elicit a response, but rather they are used for effect.

Rhetorical questions have a way of getting people excited about your subject. Here's an example of a rhetorical question that a presenter addressing a local town council started his presentation with: "Ladies and gentleman, is there any civility left in politics today?" A statement like this is bound to get the attention of any political junkie anywhere—exactly its intent! Like many of the techniques presented so far, asking a rhetorical question is as much about how it is said as what is said.

For effect, try slowing down your speech and emphasizing key words and then end with silence as you soak up the audience's reaction. Rhetorical questions are a great way to prime your audience to hear what you have to say.

Other Techniques to Engage Your Audience

As you gain more experience you may decide to include some other techniques designed to get your audience to think. Such techniques include quotations, metaphors, analogies, anecdotes, and stories. As you practice using these literary forms of expression, keep in mind that your delivery is as much a factor in its effectiveness as what you say.

Quotations

Quotations from others strategically placed in the beginning, middle, or end of your presentation often have the effect of stimulating people's thinking. Before you use a quote, though, be sure of its authenticity (especially true of anything found online) and its relevance to your subject matter. When you use a quotation, always give attribution to the appropriate source.

Metaphors

Metaphors, as well as analogies and anecdotes, are thought-provoking forms of speech that open people's minds to think differently about a subject or issue. According to *Webster's Ninth New Collegiate Dictionary* (Merriam-Webster, 1993), a metaphor is a "figure of speech in which a word or phrase literally denoting one kind of object or idea is used in place of another to suggest a likeness or analogy between them."

One presenter speaking at a career development seminar used the New York marathon as a metaphor for the effort involved in searching for a new job. As he planted a picture in the minds of his audience of the daunting task of running the marathon, he explained that conducting a job search was similar because those who are successful in completing the journey in the shortest time are always the ones who spent the most time preparing themselves.

Think About This

Paraphrasing, also called reflective listening, is a powerful facilitation tool because it helps the presenter to uncover real feelings without placing a value judgment on what the audience member is saying. You can use this form of listening in your everyday dealings with people, so practice trying to put into words not only what people are saying, but also what they are feeling whenever you have a chance. You'll be amazed at how positively people will respond, having felt truly listened to.

Analogies

An analogy, according to *Webster's*, is a "resemblance in some particulars between things otherwise unlike." Analogies, like metaphors, often help paint a picture in people's minds that help people to "see" concepts or ideas more clearly. One presenter, wanting to lay the foundation for introducing a new financial reporting system, used this analogy: "Trying to reconcile our old monthly financial reports was like putting together a jigsaw puzzle only to find some of the pieces missing." Nodding their heads in agreement, the listeners became eager, wanting to learn more about this new, less frustrating system.

Stories

Although not everyone is a storyteller, stories are an interesting and entertaining way of getting an audience's attention. Much of what we learn in our lifetime comes through stories we are told. For example, Martin Luther King used stories that helped change

Think About This

Try this nonverbal cue the next time someone in your audience responds to a question you've asked. Although the natural thing to do would be for the person to respond directly to you, by extending your arm and with a slight movement of your hand toward the audience, indicate to the speaker that he or she should speak to the audience and not just to you. This interaction gets the audience involved and takes the focus, at least for that moment, off of you and on to the point being made. Another technique for doing this is to literally move toward the person speaking and stand next to or a little behind the speaker as he or she speaks and, once again, with a slight wave of the hand or by saying, "How about telling the audience?", you can accomplish the same goal. This technique takes time to get comfortable doing and especially to look natural doing it, but once again, practice, practice, practice.

the way our country thought about the races living together, and John F. Kennedy created in people's minds a picture of a man on the moon.

Obviously these were great orators with the power to use their words to change the thinking of whole societies. In many ways, as a presenter standing before an audience, you serve as a leader; trying to get your audience to see a certain point of view, come to your way of thinking, or accept certain facts or information. Stories, also referred to as anecdotes, can be about ourselves or about others. Just as the Reverend King did when speaking about his dream for the future, telling a story as part of your presentation is an excellent way of taking something theoretical or abstract and making it real for your audience.

Basic Rule 14

A good story paints a picture in words that will last long after your audience leaves your presentation.

Using Humor

Making the decision whether to use humor in your presentation requires some thought. Making the wrong decision can ruin a perfectly good presentation. The key to making the decision is self-awareness. As mentioned previously, if you are considered to be a humorous person by people who know you and you have a way of making people laugh (or even smile a lot) when you make a quip or say a joke or something funny, then consider incorporating humor into your presentation. However, there is more of a potential downside to using humor in your presentation than an upside.

Think About This

If you are new to giving presentations, it's tough enough giving one without having to try to get your audience to laugh too. Not every presentation has to be serious, but humor should be a natural part of your presentation, and not something you drop in here and there to get a laugh. Unless being humorous is natural to you, then you might want to gain a little more experience before it becomes a part of your presentation style.

Here is the upside: People may find you witty and funny, they'll laugh, and they may even remember what you said to make them chuckle. Here is the downside: You may not be quite as humorous as you thought, or, worse, your "humor" is misinterpreted or found offensive by some, leaving a bad impression on your audience, and that's what your audience remembers instead of the important points of your presentation.

Getting It Done

The following exercise will allow you to not only revisit the major points in the chapter you just read, but you will also have the opportunity to hone your newly learned skills and actually apply them to ensure that you can use your facilitation skills in an effective way.

Exercise 4-1 is a useful checklist that will help you get ready to incorporate facilitation skills into your presentation. Complete it prior to your presentation.

Exercise 4-1. Using your facilitation skills.

1. I understand the role facilitation can play in my presentation. Yes_____ No_____.
   Jot down some notes here:

   _____

   _____

   _____

2. I feel comfortable asking open, closed, and hypothetical questions and the reasons for asking each kind. Yes_____ No_____. Jot down some notes here:

   _____

   _____

   _____

3. I understand how to incorporate a Q & A session into my presentation. Yes_____ No_____.
   Jot down your notes here:

   _____

   _____

   _____

4. I understand how to use various verbal and nonverbal skills discussed in the chapter (active listening, nonverbal cues). Yes_____ No_____. Jot down your notes here:

   _____

   _____

   _____

5. I know when to use humor in my presentation. Yes_____ No_____. Jot down some notes here:

   _____

   _____

   _____

6. I know what a rhetorical question is designed to do. Yes_____ No_____. Jot down some notes here:

    _____

    _____

    _____

7. I understand how to incorporate smooth transitions into my presentation.
    Yes_____ No_____. Jot down some notes here:

    _____

    _____

    _____

8. I understand the importance of using silence as a facilitation technique.
    Yes_____ No_____. Jot down some notes here:

    _____

    _____

    _____

9. I am familiar with the use of metaphors, analogies, and stories as part of my presentation.
    Yes_____ No_____. Jot down some notes here:

    _____

    _____

    _____

    _____

Ensuring a really great presentation means taking care of the details. In chapter 5 you'll learn how to set an environment that allows for maximum learning while keeping your audience comfortable.

5

Setting the Right Environment

■ ■

 What's Inside This Chapter

Here, you'll see how to:

▶ Take care of the details that make for a successful presentation

▶ Make your room's environment just right for your audience

▶ Determine the best setup for your room

▶ Ensure that your room's size is conducive to meeting your audience's needs

▶ Choose the most appropriate audiovisual aids for your presentation

▶ Set the stage for success by getting the lay of the land

It's all too easy to fall into the trap of spending much of your time preparing your presentation and forgetting to plan the right kind of atmosphere to make it successful. An easy way to remember the importance of creating a proper atmosphere is to treat the room you'll be presenting in as if it is your living room where guests will be visiting. Certainly you wouldn't have company over without going out of your way to make your house look inviting and feel comfortable.

If you have some difficulty accepting the analogy between your presentation room and a living room, here's something most can understand: the value of maintaining control over a situation where your professionalism will be evaluated by others. Because it is you giving the presentation, it is in your best interest to exercise as much control as you can over what happens around you to ensure your presentation's success. Control means being just as concerned with issues like how the room is set up and whether people will be able to see and hear you as you are about preparing to give your presentation.

Think About This

By taking responsibility for any situation, you are better able to control the outcome. Although giving a presentation is not a life-and-death matter, your credibility is always at stake. You never want to get into a situation where you risk blowing the time and effort you spent preparing your presentation because you or someone you were relying on for support failed to come through. Remember, it's one thing to have a wonderful presentation prepared, and another if your audience can't hear you from the back of the room.

It's important to assume a certain amount of responsibility for the logistical part of your presentation. How much responsibility is involved depends on the nature of the presentation, but there are some basic issues that are important to address no matter what form your presentation takes. Take care of the details, and the big things will take care of themselves.

It's Always About You

To be successful you need to assume some responsibility for taking care of the details involved in your presentation. However, you don't have to go it alone. It helps to have friends who can assist you with setting up the room, catering the food, providing the audiovisual equipment, and managing the facility. All these functions have an important role in making your presentation—and you—a success. Make a special effort to be respectful and courteous to people who can affect your success not only because it's the professional thing to do, but because they have the potential to make or break your presentation just by the quality of services they provide.

Basic Rule 15

Taking care of the details before your presentation will give you the time to focus on giving your presentation and meeting your audience's needs.

To help ensure that your presentation proceeds exactly the way you want it to, start at the beginning with the basics, making sure you are clear about the following information:

☑ *Time:* Know exactly what time your presentation is to be given, and plan to arrive at least 15–30 minutes early to check out the room and other logistical considerations.

☑ *Date:* It's easy to forget the date of the same presentation you've done over and over for different audiences at your company, so don't take a chance with ruining your credibility by failing to showing up when you are supposed to.

☑ *Location:* Know the exact location of your presentation. Even if it's in the building you work in, check it out ahead of time. If it's off site, get directions for getting there, and plan your arrival with enough time available to make any changes or correct any problems that might exist. If it's in an area you are unfamiliar with, know how long it should take to get to your destination including any potential areas for delay.

Presentation Room

Every room you give a presentation in is different in some way and presents unique challenges. That's why you must express your wants and needs, if you have a say in where you will give your presentation. When you are offered different options about where and how your presentation will take place, never

Think About This

A theme throughout this book is that audiences are usually forgiving of presenters when they falter if the audience believes the presenter was otherwise prepared and tried his or her best. This axiom is especially true for less-experienced presenters because many audience members envision themselves in the same situation and can empathize with the work put into giving a presentation. Most audiences, though, do not tolerate carelessness, which usually indicates being unprepared, or worse, a lack of respect.

say (or think, for that matter), "Don't worry about me, any place is fine." If you have some control over the logistics of the room, take advantage of this opportunity to create an atmosphere that makes you feel comfortable and will best meet your audience's needs. You may find many of those details already taken care of for you, but there are still several things you can do to help ensure that your presentation will be a rousing success, among them room setup and the environment.

Room Setup

There is no single way to set up a room for a presentation. Because some setups work better for certain kinds of presentations, don't be shy about expressing your desire in the way the room will be set up. Table 5-1 lists the most common room setups, as well as when each works and doesn't work. Each setup is then described in more detail in the sections that follow.

Rounds. Some also refer to this room configuration as pods. Actually, the term *rounds,* referring to the shape of the tables that are used, is a bit of a misnomer because the tables can also be square or rectangular. In figure 5-1 the rounds and accompanying chairs are set up in random fashion throughout the room. The presenter is at the part of the room designated as the front, along with any audiovisual equipment, podiums,

Figure 5-1. A typical room setup involving rounds.

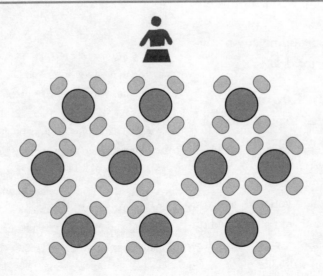

Table 5-1. Decision matrix for room set-up alternatives.

Style	When to Use	When Not to Use	Alternatives
Rounds	• Larger groups • Work in teams • Small group interaction • When using audiovisuals	• Room too small • Group less than 15	• Classroom • Chevron
Classroom	• Any size group depending on room size • When using audiovisuals • When focus is on the presenter	• You want group interaction • Room dimensions are too long or wide	• Chevron • Rounds • U-shape
U-Shape	• Smaller group size • Open environment • When using audiovisuals	• Small room • Large group • Work in teams	• Classroom • Chevron • Conference
Chevron	• Large groups • For presenters who like to move • When using visuals	• When a warm, personal atmosphere is needed	• U-shape • Rounds • Classroom
Conference	• Small group • Group discussion • Formal and intimate	• Room to spread out • Using audiovisuals that require room • Presenter movement	• Classroom • U-shape
Theater	• Large group • Focus on presenter • When using audiovisuals	• Establish intimate environment • Small group • Group interaction	• Rounds • Classroom • Chevron

or tables he or she plans to use. The number of people at each table usually ranges from four to 10, depending on the size of the table and number of people in the audience.

Rounds work well for an audience of at least 15 people, especially when you want your audience to work in small groups or teams on an exercise or game. This setup creates a friendly environment that enables those at each table to interact and mingle. On a purely practical note, the table offers a surface that makes taking notes easy. It's also fair to say that rooms large enough to support a number of rounds placed throughout can also support most audiovisual equipment. This room arrangement gives you a great deal of flexibility when it comes to choosing the best audiovisual to support your presentation.

Setting up rounds requires a room large enough to allow ample space between the tables. To cram tables in a small room with people from separate tables brushed up against one another defeats the whole purpose of this setup. This setup often requires designated people to arrange the room, so some expense is probably involved, especially at off-site locations. But, perhaps the biggest problem that rounds present is that some may need to crane their necks or turn around to see you because of the position of their chair.

Classroom Style. Classroom style is similar to the traditional school classroom setup, with rows of desks or tables and chairs all facing the presenter who is standing in front (figure 5-2).

Classroom style sets a collegial tone for a group of almost any size. A classroom setup usually allows enough room for most audiovisual equipment and is often already equipped with some low-tech aids, such as flipcharts, whiteboards, or blackboards. A real advantage of the classroom setup is that all eyes are focused on the presenter because all seats face the front.

The classroom setup is not one that enables people within the audience to interact with one another freely. Although this limitation can be resolved by moving the chairs around, it does not make for an open atmosphere as some other setups, which are geared for maximum interaction. Another disadvantage of this setup is that if the

Figure 5-2. A typical classroom setup.

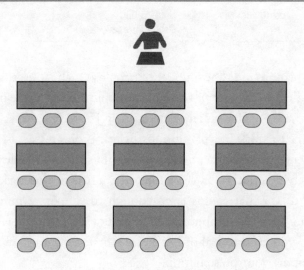

room is very long or very wide, some people in the room are likely to feel as though they are somewhere out in the hinterland—not exactly the kind of atmosphere conducive to focusing on you.

U-Shaped Configuration. This room configuration was once especially popular with those who ran group workshops because it allows people to easily see one another, and it provides ample space for the group leader to wander inside the U (figure 5-3). Although somewhat less popular now, it still offers some real benefits.

Figure 5-3. A typical U-shaped room setup.

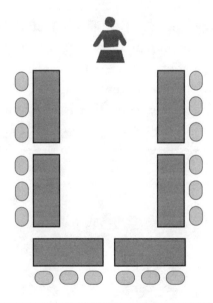

For the U-shaped setup, desks, chairs, or tables are set next to one another with a horizontal row in the back of the room and a parallel row extending to the front on either end, forming the letter U (figure 5-3). The inside of the U is open space where the presenter may stand, or he or she may opt to stand at the open end of the U. For an informal presentation, the presenter could even take a seat in one of the chairs of the U.

The U-shaped setup is great for the presenter who enjoys the freedom of walking up close to those he or she is presenting to. It is also a good choice when you wish to create an open atmosphere conducive to having groups of two or three people talking and interacting with one another. The U-shaped setup works best for groups of 12 to

24, but it can support more people if the room is wide enough. Of course, if the group is too big or too small the purpose of this setup is defeated. Most rooms that can support a U-shaped setup can accommodate most audiovisual equipment too.

Cramming a U-shaped setup of chairs and tables in a room too small may create an uncomfortable atmosphere where people have difficulty walking outside of the U to their seats, exactly the opposite of the environment you were shooting for. Another important point when choosing this setup is to recognize its limitations as it relates to size of the group. In addition, this setup usually makes it uncomfortable for group activities involving more than four or five people because only the two corners of the U make it easy for people to see and talk with one another.

Chevron. This setup combines the best features of the classroom and rounds arrangements. Like the classroom setup, rows of tables are placed one in back of the other, except in this configuration they are put at an angle, forming the letter V, usually with a walkway in the middle, as shown in figure 5-4. Like the rounds setup, it makes for easy pairing of groups or teams already set at the different tables.

Figure 5-4. A typical chevron room setup.

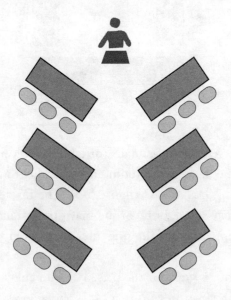

This setup offers two main benefits. First, it can accommodate large groups. With the tables set on angles, it's easier for people in the back of the room to see than with a classroom setup. Second, it allows the presenter the flexibility to walk in the space that separates the sides of the chevron. Like the classroom setup, the chevron is conducive to using a whole host of visual aids.

In terms of disadvantages, those in the back of the room, even at an angle, sometimes have difficulty seeing especially if the group is a large one. Although somewhat better than a classroom, this setup does not really create an atmosphere that is very warm or personal because everyone (except those in the front row) is looking at someone else's back.

Conference Style. This style usually involves the audience sitting in chairs around a large conference table. The presenter can take a seat at the table, either at the head for a stronger presence or at any chair for a more informal effect (figure 5-5). Conference style seating can be accommodated in a rich setting like a boardroom, or it can be used at a large table in the cafeteria where small groups tend to meet to hear the latest updates on a number of subjects.

Conference style works well for both formal and informal presentations where the audience is relatively small, depending on the size of the room. This is an ideal setup if your intent is to add some importance to the presentation (boardroom) by

Figure 5-5. A typical conference room setup.

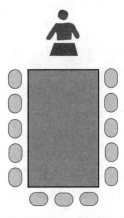

bringing people into a setting that is intimate and conducive to a personal presentation and discussion. In these situations the audience usually enjoys comfortable chairs and a nice large table to take notes on.

As intimate a space as most conference rooms are, taken to the extreme they can become a cramped place if the room is too small to accommodate the size of the group. Conference style can also limit your choice of audiovisual aids. Presenters who like to walk around the room may find that this setup confines them to one end of the table. If you are planning to do some team or group activities, people won't be able to spread out because everyone is seated at a single, large table.

Theater. Theater (sometimes called auditorium) usually refers to seating in a large room with fixed seats that cannot be moved. This arrangement usually dictates a lack of flexibility for the presenter in terms of arranging the room.

Theater setup works very well for large groups where the focus is on the presenter and not on audience interaction. Another reason this is an excellent choice is that it usually offers the presenter the full gamut of audiovisual options from which to choose. Although theater setup is usually synonymous with more formal presentations, if the presenter is equipped with a cordless microphone, the atmosphere can quickly become informal even with a very large group, as the presenter is free to move around the room and interact with the audience members.

This is not the room setup for you if you want an intimate and warm atmosphere. It's not that it can't be, but it takes a great deal of skill, experience, and practice to make a large room feel warm. If a large theater space is booked for a presentation to a small group, the room looks absolutely cavernous, and people may sit at some distance from each other, eliminating any possibility of interaction without your having to ask them to move in. Theater setup usually precludes note taking by the audience members unless the seats are equipped with folding desktop surfaces.

Room Setup Crisis!

If you walk into a room that is not set up the way you are expecting, you have some decisions to make about what you will do. First, check the time remaining before your presentation is scheduled to begin. If you have arrived early enough to make some changes, will it be worth the effort? Make your decision based on your answers to these two questions:

1. Will I be so adversely affected by this room setup that it will prevent me from meeting my goals for the presentation?
2. Will my audience be so adversely affected by this room setup that it will prevent them from benefiting from the presentation?

If the answer is yes to either of these questions, enlist some help and try to approximate the room setup you need. However, if the answer to both questions is no or if you do not have enough time, make whatever minor changes you can and focus on making your presentation a memorable one despite this obstacle.

You can make minor adjustments as you go along. Maintain a lighthearted attitude; infuse a little humor into the situation, if appropriate. Keep in the back of your mind that audiences are more willing to give you the benefit of the doubt if everything is not perfect if you are professional, prepared, and confident as you confront the little issues that often come up during the presentation. Remember—it's still about your audience needs and your ability to meet them.

Basic Rule 16

If your audience isn't comfortable in the environment you've set, it will be less apt to listen to what you have to say. Work toward a room setup that works best for both you and your audience.

The Environment

Size. When it comes to making a presentation, the size of the room is important. By knowing the size of the room beforehand you can plan better for your presentation. The two most important considerations are knowing that everyone will be able to see and hear you and being sure that they will be comfortable doing so. If potential problems exist, it's better that you know about them beforehand so you'll be in a position to resolve them ahead of time.

For example if you'll be using audiovisual equipment, determine whether the room can accommodate the ones you've decided to use. Ask your sponsor or, if possible, visit the room before your presentation to help you decide. Do these checks to prevent arriving at the room and finding that the overhead projector you were planning to use is so big that it will prevent some people from seeing the image projected on the wall.

Guard against the mistake made by many new presenters (and even some experienced ones) when they think that the visual aid you are most comfortable using is appropriate for every room. That's not true, as some red-faced presenters have found as they realize too late that half the audience can't read the beautiful, printed flipcharts that took so much time to create.

Some presenters are movers and shakers; that is, they enjoy the freedom of being able to move around the room during their presentations. If that's you, find out what the room dimensions are and any obstructions ahead of time that might restrict your movement. Once again, a talk with your sponsor or a quick visit to the room will give you the information you need. Such a limitation might not necessitate a major change in your presentation, but who needs surprises?

Temperature. Because room temperatures can vary widely, you'll want to try to make sure that you and your audience will be comfortable. At some point before your presentation, investigate whether the room has a thermostat. If so, check the temperature, and determine whether it can be adjusted if need be. If the room temperature feels fine, chances are it will not be a problem during your presentation and you have one less thing to worry about. If, however, the temperature is outside your comfort zone before your presentation, think about what effect it will have on both you and your audience during your presentation.

If you can't adjust the temperature setting, find out who can and get it fixed. The last thing you want is your audience bundling up because it's too cold or nodding off because it's too warm. Here are some guidelines to follow:

- ▶ Set the thermostat for a comfortable level, depending on the season, size of the room, and the audience.
- ▶ If the room is a bit on the cool side, that's probably desirable because the room will automatically warm up a few degrees because of the body heat generated when it's full.
- ▶ Keep the room somewhat cooler if your audience is likely to be wearing business suits, which are often made of wool.
- ▶ For a daytime presentation in a room with windows, consider the effect of sunlight on the room temperature. Adjust the curtains or blinds, and perhaps the thermostat, accordingly.
- ▶ If you are someone who still wears sweaters in July or short sleeves in the middle of the winter, it might be wise to have a colleague determine the best room temperature.

Lighting. Lighting is an important factor to consider as you are creating a comfortable environment for your audience. Room lighting also can influence the effectiveness of some visual aids you might use, your audience's ability to take notes, and the mood for your presentation.

It's important to know beforehand how your presentation might be affected by the lighting in your room and your ability to control it. This factor is especially important if you are going to use any visual aid—slides or transparencies, for example—requiring adjustment of the lights. For example, if you are using slides, you may need to arrange with an audience member or support person to draw the shades before you lower the lights.

If you must take lighting into account for your presentation, consider these guidelines:

▶ Find out what the lighting options are in your presentation room either by asking your sponsor or visiting the room yourself.

▶ Start by locating the lighting controls for all the lights in the room, and practice using dimmer and slide switches.

▶ Once you're better acquainted with the room, determine what, if any, adjustments you'll need to make, and arrange with the appropriate people before your presentation to get them taken care of.

▶ If necessary, arrange to have someone sit close to the lighting controls so that you can ask him or her to change the lighting at different parts of your presentation and explain exactly what you want done and when.

Noise Level. The level of noise outside your room can affect your presentation, especially when presenting at a hotel or conference center. It's wise to check the room before your presentation to determine the outside noise level. Check to see how thin the partitions are and take note of the proximity of the kitchen or other noisy areas.

If you suspect that there might be a problem, consider raising your concerns with your sponsor or facility representative to address the issue. If the situation is likely to interfere with your presentation and cannot be ameliorated, consider asking for another room. After all, it's you up there speaking and on the line.

Audiovisual Aids

Chances are you'll use at least one audiovisual aid to support your presentation. Audiovisual aids can make a bland presentation exciting, but they can also turn a good presentation into a disaster if the presenter has not adequately planned for their use. Therefore, it's especially important that appropriate accommodations be made for any audiovisual aid you decide to use. As part of your plan, make sure that you have accounted for the following provisions when using audiovisual aids prior to your presentation:

▶ Be sure there are enough outlets to accommodate your audiovisual equipment; know the location of each; and arrange for necessary extension cords or power strips.

▶ Ensure that any cords or wires are taped down or covered to eliminate tripping and electrical hazards.

▶ Familiarize yourself with each piece of equipment before your presentation. Yes, this means you might have to open an instruction manual!

▶ Develop a contingency plan if some equipment malfunctions. Locate replacement parts, such as bulbs and batteries. Figure out what you'll do if you are forced to conduct your presentation without any audiovisual aids.

▶ Identify the on-site audiovisual support person, and find out how to contact him or her if needed.

▶ Carry your own presenter's toolkit of audiovisual-related items, including Magic Markers, a grease pencil, extra bulbs, and transparencies in the event that these supplies are not available on site.

Think About This

Here's a tip that will make life a little easier: Too often conference centers, hotels, or your own organization provide markers that are nearly dried up or are toxic with overpowering smell. Purchase your own markers so that you have a set of different colors to take with you when you present. Try buying nontoxic, water-based markers in various colors. Not only do they have a pleasant smell, but the ink can be washed out of your clothes in the event of an accident.

Lecterns and Tables

A lectern is a small desk that usually sits on a podium or table where you can rest your presentation notes. It would not be unusual to find yourself speaking from behind a lectern if you were making a formal presentation. Besides the obvious advantage of having a place to rest your notes hidden away from your audience, the lectern can be a special comfort to less-experienced presenters, who may feel the need to be anchored to something while giving their presentation. Unfortunately, this same benefit when taken to the extreme can be a liability if presenters grasp the lectern so tightly that they look scared to let go.

An ordinary card table or a long conference table can serve as a lectern or podium. For informal presentations it's often wise to ask for an appropriate size table to rest your notes, transparencies, handouts, and any other materials you'll need during your presentation. Although not as impressive looking as a lectern, a table sometimes works better because it

Think About This

Very often, lecterns come with a built-in light, a microphone, or both. The light is especially helpful in darker rooms. However, when using a microphone attached to a lectern, it pays to test the microphone before you give your presentation to know how to position yourself behind it for the best sound quality and to find a good height so that it's not poking you in the eye when you speak from behind it.

provides more room to spread notes and materials on and is less of a barrier between you and your audience. If needed, also arrange beforehand to have extra tables set up to put handouts, books, or other materials on.

Food and Breaks

These days it seems as though making a presentation and eating go hand in hand, so it's not unusual for there to be coffee, juice, pastries, fruit, or other snacks available at a presentation you are giving. You may even be asked to give a presentation over lunch, where more substantial fare, such as sandwiches or even hot meals, is to be served. Evening presentations can sometimes involve full-course dinners or buffets. In any case, food service can affect your presentation, so, if you have some say about the situation, you may wish to consider these suggestions:

▶ Get to know the people who are handling the food service, and be clear about what your expectations are regarding the kinds of food that will be served, and when, how, and where the food will be set up.

▶ Opt for lighter, nutritious fare, such as fruit, pasta, salads, and small sandwiches. Heavier food tends to make people drowsy, especially right after lunch or late in the afternoon. Have plenty of bottled water and juices, as an alternative to sodas, as well as both decaffeinated and caffeinated coffee and tea.

▸ If you have a choice, ask that the food service be set up in advance, so that the clanking of dishes and glasses doesn't interfere with your presentation. If this is not practical, try to have the food set up outside the presentation room to minimize any disturbance.

Although you may not have any say about will be served, you do have control over what you ingest so remember to:

▸ Eat and drink lightly before your presentation. Water and juices work well, as do fruits, light salads, and pasta.
▸ Keep away from alcohol because any upside is far outweighed by the downside.
▸ Moderate the caffeine you ingest; after the jolt often come the jitters.
▸ Drink water. It's the best thing for getting rid of dry mouth, but don't drink too much for obvious reasons.
▸ Don't eat messy food or drink something that might stain your clothes if spilled.

Think About This

If you don't want to find yourself apologizing to your audience, check, check, and double-check all essential aspects of your presentation. Wherever you are dependent on others to help ensure your success, don't consider yourself a pest if you have an issue that you think needs to be addressed prior to your presentation.

The Lay of the Land

When you arrive early at your presentation room, you have a chance to walk around to view things from the audience's perspective from different vantage points. That way, you can fine-tune your presentation to ensure that the audience's needs are met. As you walk around the room, visualize making your presentation and anticipate the reaction you will be getting. For many presenters changes in their presentations often start by visualizing a virtual scenario and picturing how it could be better. It's one thing to do this while practicing at home or in your office, but it's quite another when you do it in the actual room you will be presenting in.

The Details

Some details of preparation might be overlooked, especially if you find yourself paying too much attention to some of the big issues. If not addressed, though, these little things taken together can have a detrimental effect on your presentation. Some of the details you should consider are your introduction, your attire, and a title for your presentation.

Introductions

If you know you are to be introduced before your presentation, consider writing the introduction yourself to maintain control over what's said about you. You can either ask the person introducing you to read it verbatim or use it to craft some notes that he or she will use when introducing you.

Attire

If you are unsure about what the appropriate dress is for your presentation, ask your sponsor. Get clarity around the mysterious "casual business" attire, so that your casual is the same as everyone else's casual. For business attire, men should wear jackets and ties, and women cannot go wrong with a conservative business suit. For formal presentations both women and men should keep their jackets on and buttoned while presenting. You have much more leeway with informal presentations. Remember, you want the audience to remember you and what you said, not what you wore.

Presentation Title

If you're asked to supply a title for your presentation that will be used for some publicity beforehand, take full advantage of this opportunity to come up with something that will grab people's attention. Use words that connote action and state the benefit of attending. Be creative within the context of the subject matter and the make-up of the audience and be careful of making promises that you cannot keep.

Evaluation

To grow and improve as a presenter it's important to ask for and receive feedback from both your audience and sponsor. If you decide to use a formal evaluation, consider dividing it into content-related and presenter-related questions. Often, asking questions and providing a five-point scale with room for comments is all you need to get some feedback on how you did. Isolated comments, both positive and negative, should be taken with a grain of salt. A pattern of scores and comments, however, is usually a good indication of how well your presentation went. Incorporate the feedback you receive into the development of your next presentation, and always work toward continual learning and improvement.

To ease your mind, remember that things sometimes go wrong, no matter how hard you try to prevent problems. That's when your decision-making and problem-solving skills are put to the test. Focus on solving the big problems that may prevent you from achieving your goals and meeting your audience's needs. Draw upon your professionalism, preparation, and support from others—including your audience—to get past the smaller challenges.

Getting It Done

The following exercise will allow you to not only revisit the major points in the chapter you just read, but also to hone your newly learned skills and apply them to ensure an appropriate presentation environment. Exercise 5-1 is a useful checklist to help you get ready to set an appropriate environment for your presentation. Complete it prior to your presentation.

Exercise 5-1. Preparing the right environment for the presentation.

1. I have evaluated and chosen the best room setup for my presentation.
   Yes_____ No_____. Jot down your notes here:

   _____

   _____

   _____

2. I understand the pros and cons of this room setup and am prepared to make the necessary adjustments to ensure my presentation's success.
   Yes_____ No_____. Jot down your notes here:

   _____

   _____

   _____

3. I have visited the room or have asked my sponsor about the room and am familiar with its layout. Yes_____ No_____. Jot down your notes here:

_____

_____

_____

4. I have chosen my audiovisual equipment for my program and have checked to ensure that my room can accommodate my choices. Yes_____ No_____. Jot down your notes here:

_____

_____

_____

5. I have considered other important factors such as the following:

   ☐ I know how to get to the location of my presentation.

   ☐ I know what time the presentation is.

   ☐ I know whom to contact if I have any questions before or during my presentation.

   ☐ I've made sure my attire is appropriate.

   ☐ I've checked into food and beverage service.

   ☐ I know how to control the lighting in the room.

   ☐ The temperature in the room will be comfortable for me and my audience.

People remember what they see as well as what they hear. Knowing what audiovisual aids are appropriate for your presentation and how to use them are critical to your success as a presenter. In the next chapter you'll look at the most common audiovisual aids to choose from and see how to select the right ones for your presentation.

Choosing and Using Audiovisual Aids

What's Inside This Chapter

Here, you'll see how to:

▶ Recognize the five myths of choosing audiovisual aids

▶ Determine the right way to create and use a flipchart and easel

▶ Discover when and how to create and use overhead transparencies

▶ Find out how to make the best use of videotape and DVD

▶ Learn about the advantages of using photographic or computer-generated slides for your presentation

▶ Decide whether to take the big step toward computer-generated visuals

▶ Learn how to increase your presentation's effectiveness with visual props

▶ Choose and use the best microphone for your presentation

You have a presentation to do. That's great! You've been asked to make your presentation interesting, informative, and entertaining. That's a challenge! You're thinking visuals, but should you use a flipchart or transparencies or the latest computer-generated gizmo? The answer to this question is: It depends. This chapter is designed to help you formulate an answer based on your particular presentation circumstance. Toward the end of the chapter, you'll find table 6-1, which compares the features, advantages, and disadvantages of each type of audiovisual described here.

The Myths

First, let's start by dispelling some commonly accepted myths about the use of visual aids. Here are five myths you're likely to encounter:

▶ *Myth 1: The more visual aids I use the better.* Not so. The use of visual aids should *support* your presentation and not *be* your presentation. Beginners (and some experienced presenters, too) get into trouble by overdoing visual aids to the point that the message gets lost in the visual. In addition, the presenter can end up spending valuable time reading the visuals and not facilitating learning. Here's a rule of thumb: The best presentations tend to have a mix of delivery methods that use both verbal and nonverbal techniques, as well as the appropriate visual aids to support the presenter's message.

▶ *Myth 2: Any visual aid is better than none.* Not true. A visual aid that is too complex to understand or poorly produced is often such a turnoff to an audience that it probably would be better to use no visual aid at all. Visual aids should reinforce learning while being easy to understand and of high quality.

▶ *Myth 3: The more high-tech the visual aid used in your presentation, the better.* Untrue. Sure, the use of the latest computer-generated gizmo can dazzle your audience and be a great support to your presentation, but when all is said and done, an effective presentation is still about the message. If the message gets lost in the razzle-dazzle, then the dazzle is not worth very much. Use the most effective visual aids to support the learning

▶ *Myth 4: More things can go wrong when using a visual aid in your presentation, so it's better to just rely on yourself.* False. This may sound like the complete opposite of myth 1, but the point is that most problems are usually due to a lack of preparation. Sure, things can happen that all the preparation in the world can't prevent. The important thing is to check and double-check your equipment and the visuals themselves. In addition, your presenter's toolkit can save the day if technology fails you. Just make sure you can access a fresh pad of flipchart paper, an easel, and some colorful markers. If you are prepared and have done all you can do to expect the unexpected, then your presentation will go just fine. Your professionalism and the support of your audience will save the day!

▶ *Myth 5: Visual aids cost too much.* Not necessarily so. It's true that some technologically based aids, especially those that are computer generated, can be costly. By using templates, basic programs, and a good cost-effective printing company, you can produce high-quality visuals while being cost effective. The important thing to remember is that the quality of visual aids reflects the quality of the program.

Audiovisual Aids: The Basics and Beyond

Most readers of this book are looking for the basics of presentation. In the traditional training world, *the basics* means flipcharts and overhead transparencies. You can also use visual props and handouts to support your presentation. Now, trainers have myriad high-tech options from which to choose: videotape, digital versatile discs (DVDs), photographic slides, and digital slides. Believe it or not, it's possible to download a PowerPoint presentation to your personal digital assistant (PDA), which can then interface via a special accessory to a digital projector. That way, you don't even need to carry a laptop computer to project digital slides! So, how do you select the right audiovisual aid for your presentation?

It's important to remember that despite all the amazing technology available for presentations, most presentations made still rely on effective use of low-tech, basic presentation tools. Besides, if you are not very familiar with your chosen presentation technology or you if have chosen technology over substance, you may be doing yourself more harm than good.

With that cautionary note sounded, this section first describes the most commonly available and least technology-driven visual aids and then progresses toward more complex, technology-driven visual aids.

Basic Rule 17
Don't get caught up in all the audiovisual hype. Remember that audiovisuals are just for support and should never be the whole show.

Flipchart and Easel

A flipchart is the most basic aid in a presenter's visual toolbox. They usually measure 27 by 34 inches and consist of large pads of paper attached to a stand or set upon an easel. You can purchase flipcharts that are colored, lined, or imprinted with graph gridlines, although the standard issue is white. Some pads are made like giant Post-it notes that can be torn off and temporarily pasted on a wall. If your room is extremely small, you may be able to use a specially designed flipchart that's small enough to fit right on a conference table.

Think About This

The terms *flipchart* and *easel* are sometimes used interchangeably, so make sure you are clear when you are communicating with a hotel coordinator or your organization's audiovisual team about your need for a flipchart, easel, or both. Don't assume that "everyone knows" that you need both because many a presenter has arrived at his or her destination only to find one without the other.

When to Use a Flipchart. Flipcharts are the most basic of training and presentation tools. Even poor handwriting cannot be considered an excuse for not using a flipchart, although you should do your best to write legibly. Consider using flipcharts when:

▶ *Your presentation is informal.* Although flipcharts can be produced professionally, most presenters are capable of making an effective flipchart with a little effort. Informal settings, such as a weekly sales meeting, probably can be handled just fine with a series of flipcharts as your visual aid.

▶ *Participants' numbers and the room size are appropriate for flipchart use.* Eight participants in a room that's, say, 10 feet by 15 feet make a flipchart an obvious choice. Moreover, when you use a flipchart in such an intimate setting, you create an open, personal environment for your audience.

▶ *Your presentation is in the late afternoon.* Flipcharts offer a special advantage for late afternoon events. It's not necessary to dim the lights as you would for a slide presentation; that way, you may be able to deter your audience from catching a catnap.

▶ *You have little time or no budget.* Clearly, a flipchart is the perfect choice of a visual aid when you have to give a last-minute presentation or if you have a shoestring budget for your presentation. You can create hand-drawn graphs, charts, and other visuals that will get your point across without blowing your budget.

▶ *You want the ability to create visuals on the fly during your presentation.* Flipcharts allow you to mark up preprinted pages with comments and thoughts. Of course, you can mark up an overhead transparency on the fly and even have this flexibility with some high-tech solutions, but if your audience is small, you are in a hurry, or if you have a budget issue, flipcharts can be the answer to your presentation needs.

▶ *You plan to generate part of the presentation information on the visual aid itself during the actual presentation.* Flipcharts are very effective when you plan to gather participants' comments and contributions and write them yourself, or when participants work together to produce comments or contributions.

▶ *You want to keep multiple visuals visible to the group throughout the presentation.* When participants need to refer back to a previously presented chart or when you want to document progress during the presentation, keeping flipcharts visible on the wall is effective.

When Not to Use Flipcharts. The temporary, on-the-spot, and informal nature of the flipchart makes it ideal for some situations, but not all. For example, don't use flipcharts when:

▶ *The size of the room or the audience is not appropriate.* Although you'd think that this is an obvious point, you've probably witnessed someone writing on a flipchart in a room of 200 people. Writing on a 27-by-34-inch sheet of paper in front of an audience of this size is pretty useless. Pick another way to show your visuals—slides (traditional slide projector or digital projector) or even overhead transparencies.

▶ *You want to appear more formal and professional.* If you are presenting to a new client, a nicely executed set of color visuals, such as professionally produced transparencies or PowerPoint slides, is far better than a flipchart, which tends to be more informal in nature.

▶ *If people can't read your writing.* Face it: Some people have terrible handwriting. If there's a glimmer of hope for your handwriting, try flipchart paper formatted like graph paper. Printing with block letters using as a guide the gridlines on this type of paper can help keep even the poorest handwriting in line. If you cannot write in a reasonably legible way, you may have to consider another visual aid, such as preprinted transparencies. Here's the bottom line, though: If you choose not to have flipcharts in your repertoire because of penmanship issues, you are depriving yourself—and your audience—of a very useful and unique visual aid.

▶ *You present the same program regularly.* Of course, it doesn't make sense to write the same information again and again. You can create perfect flipcharts and have them laminated, but that can be an expensive process. An alternative is to create permanent photographic slides or to generate a PowerPoint presentation using your laptop computer and a digital projector. After all, low-tech will only take you so far.

Flipchart Basics. If you're really interested in how to create better flipcharts, whole books are available on this subject (chapter 9). But, for the purposes of this book, here are some basic guidelines for creating flipcharts:

▶ Use a maximum of six lines per page. Use only eight to 10 words per point, and use key words or phrases instead of full sentences. Remember, a busy flipchart clouds the message.

▶ Make your letters at least two inches high. Always create a mockup to check before your presentation to make sure that everyone in the room will be able to read the flipchart.

▶ Use headings on each page to differentiate among major points and set the text apart from any graphics. For example, you can use bullets, caps, boldface, different colors, underlining, different-sized letters, or some combination thereof to draw distinctions and make certain points stand out.

▶ Use three or four different colors to make your flipcharts eye-catching and easy to read. Don't go overboard with the colors, though. Too many colors will make your flipchart difficult to read. Use nontoxic, water-based markers because they smell better, won't bleed through onto walls and tables, and won't ruin your clothes.

▶ Use colors that are easy for your audience to see; black and blue tend to be the most visible. Use your judgment about using green and red for emphasis: These are great colors to imply "do" and "don't" in your text, but some audience members might be colorblind and unable to make the distinction.

▶ Choose an appropriate pad. If your handwriting needs help, then try graph paper pads. Even if you have good handwriting, these pads are easier to write on and read.

▶ Because flipchart paper is thin, leave a blank page between each written page so your audience won't be able to see each subsequent page. Attach the printed and blank pages together with a paper clip, piece of tape or staple, so that you get the full effect of the double sheet of paper, but you'll only have to flip "one" connected page rather than mess around with two.

▶ Write lightly in pencil, at the top corner of each page closest to where you will be standing, a brief heading of what's on the next page with an arrow under it. This note will help you segue seamlessly to the material on the following page.

▶ Number each page of your flipchart, then mark the corresponding number down in your notes to help you get back on track if you lose your place. If you do get a little lost with which flipchart to use you'll know exactly where to go to get back on track.

▶ Use bullets for each point you are making. Try creating bullets in different colors than the corresponding writing. To make perfect-looking bullets, some presenters use round, colorful stickers.

▶ Always check the spelling on your flipchart.

▶ Use Post-it notes or clear tape to form tabs at the side of each sheet to make it easy to find the one you want and flip open the chart to that point. The tab can be put on the page before the sheet you want or on that sheet itself. You can write the topic on the tab so you'll know the location of each page.

Now that you have been introduced to the basics of creating flipcharts, keep in mind some important things about how to effectively use the flipchart during your presentation.

You may wish to try the "touch, turn, talk" method of presenting when using your flipchart. To do this, you lightly touch the flipchart page you are referring to or write something on it before speaking, turn toward the audience, and then speak. Remember to speak to your audience, not to your flipchart.

Stand to one side of your flipchart. Which side will depend on which hand you write with. If you are right-handed, stand on the left side of the chart (as the audience faces it), and write with your right hand on the chart. If you are using tabs, place them on the left side of the pages (again, as the audience faces the chart). If you are left-handed, reverse this stance and tab placement. If you subconsciously step in front of the flipchart, you'll probably notice people craning their necks to see around you. Move!

Don't read word for word from your flipchart. Your audience members can read for themselves. Think of each page as an outline containing talking points that you will elaborate upon. You can lightly pencil notes of the content you want to cover directly on the chart at each stage of the outline, and thus use the chart as an organizer for your talk. The best presenters look natural while using any visual aid and they do not allow the visual aid to *be* the presentation.

Overhead Transparencies

The second most-used audiovisual is the overhead transparency. Sometimes these easy-to-use visuals are referred to simply as overheads, transparencies, foils, or acetates.

The rationale for using transparencies is similar to the logic for using flipcharts. Transparencies are easy to use, low-tech, and can be set up in a hurry. You can easily use colors to highlight important words or points and make these decisions on the fly. Neither flipcharts nor transparencies have to be professionally produced to be effective although they can be. Transparencies do, however, require a projector, a projection screen, and electricity, so they are definitely a step up from flipcharts on the technology scale.

Some overhead projectors can project plain paper onto a screen—no transparencies needed. Keep this capability in mind as you prepare for your presentation. Also, make sure that you find out what kind of projector will be available before you show up to make your presentation. This foreknowledge can save you from embarrassment and undue stress.

When to Use Transparencies. As noted earlier, transparencies share some of the advantages and disadvantages of flipcharts. You may wish to consider using transparencies when:

Think About This

Why ask your audience for responses if you're just going to bury them behind the next page in your flipchart? Consider posting completed flipcharts on the wall as you take responses from your audience. Just make sure to label each sheet. You might also want to post a separate sheet to write down issues that arise during your presentation.

▶ *Your presentation is informal.* Your audience probably expects your presentation to be informal when you're using transparencies, but transparencies can be made professionally if they suit your purpose and the technology you have available to you.

▶ *Your presentation is in a small room.* Sometimes transparencies work best, even better than flipcharts, if you are worried about everyone in the audience being able to see.

▶ *Your budget is small or time is short.* Transparencies can be made easily and more cheaply than slides.

▶ *You wish to project existing materials to a group.* Some transparencies are compatible with inkjet or laser printers, so you

Think About This

As you likely know, transparencies are made of clear acetate, and they tend to stick together. Although they are slightly more expensive and bulkier to store, some transparencies are framed with lightweight cardboard or heavy paper to prevent this annoyance. You can also write notes on the paper borders to serve as presentation cues. Other transparencies have a plastic edge and are three-hole punched, making them easier to grip and store. Another option is to keep transparencies in clear plastic page protectors that have blank space on the edges for notes. When you write on the transparency, you are actually writing on the page protector and it will protect your transparency from multiple cleanings.

can copy or print from your computer an organizational chart, graphic, or a photograph directly onto a transparency. Other transparencies can be loaded right into photocopiers, so you can project printed materials or even a paragraph from a book. If you take advantage of this feature, though, keep in mind type sizes of the material you're projecting, and don't put too much information on a single transparency.

▶ *You want the option of adding to your presentation on the fly.* You can use a grease pencil or a transparency marker to write or emphasize your point. Transparencies make this easy and effective.

▶ *You will be making the same presentation over and over again.* Transparencies have a reusability advantage—even better than flipcharts and they are easier to take care of and transport. Some transparencies come in a three-hole punch format, so you can organize and store them in binders.

Think About This

Using transparencies requires a bit more skill than turning a page on a flipchart, so you need to practice placing the transparency on the overhead projector screen, making sure that the image is projected face up. When you place the transparency on the glass, look behind you immediately to check placement, then continue. As you slide one sheet off, slide the next one on. It is also sometimes desirable to slide the transparency up or down to keep the item of interest near the center or the top of the screen. That way, those in the back of the room will have an easier time seeing things over the heads of those in front.

When Not to Use Overheads. Of course, overheads have their disadvantages, too. Don't use overheads if:

▸ *Your room is too small to contain a projector, a screen, and the audience.* Despite modern optics, overhead projectors are somewhat bulky and can interfere with the audience's line of vision.
▸ *You're making a formal presentation.* Transparencies are usually considered a step up in quality from the flipchart, especially when you have them professionally produced. Still, a formal presentation probably requires that you avoid the low-tech stigma and move up to slides or PowerPoint.

Overhead Transparency Basics. You'll be able to make effective use of transparencies in your presentations if you keep some of these guidelines in your mind as you create your transparencies:

▸ More is not always better. Keep the information on the transparency to a maximum of six lines and eight words per line on each transparency.
▸ If you use your computer and printer (or a photocopier) to make transparencies, remember to use type sizes large enough for your audience to see (at least a 24-point font size). Choose a clear, easy-to-read typeface or font. Principles for using color are the same as for flipcharts.
▸ Make your transparencies visually interesting by incorporating graphics, art, and icons as appropriate. This task is especially easy when you are using a computer to create your transparencies.
▸ Use headings on each page to differentiate among major points, for example, use boldface type or all caps for your headings. Try to be consistent throughout all the transparencies for a presentation.

▶ Keep some special transparency markers in your presenter's toolkit. Not all markers are equal when it comes to writing on transparencies; test them before you use them for a presentation.

▶ Number each transparency on the border, as well as on the actual transparency. You'll be glad you did if ever you drop your transparencies.

▶ Check your spelling—an important but often overlooked suggestion.

Think About This

Remember to take into consideration the size of the audience, as well as the room. It's one thing to be typing your text on your computer using a type size that looks nice and large, but that's not necessarily what it's going to look like when projected on screen. So, if you have any question about this, make sure you test things first. Incidentally, this advice also applies for the typeface you use. Use a simple, easy-to-read, sans serif font, such as Arial or Tahoma. Be consistent to maintain a professional look.

Okay, now that you have your transparencies in hand, here are a few pointers about how to use them effectively for your presentation:

▶ Before your presentation, ensure that the projector is focused so that your audience can see the entire image clearly. If you want to check the focus without revealing any of your content, place a coin with ridged edges (quarter or dime) or a ring on the glass and adjust the focus.

▶ In small rooms, consider a corner projection rather than straight forward. Your room setup would have to be adjusted to accommodate this arrangement.

▶ The fan of an overhead projector is often noisy; you may find that you have to speak up a bit to project your voice over the fan's noise.

▶ Tape the projector cord to the floor if it presents a tripping hazard.

▶ Keep your transparencies and the projector's surface clean; every bit of dust is magnified hundreds of times when it's projected onto the screen.

▶ Don't talk to the overhead projector as you describe the information on the transparency. And, don't talk to the screen either—talk to your audience. If you want to point out something on the transparency, use a pointer to point to the item *on the projector glass,* not on the screen behind you.

▶ Use a pencil or a similar object as a pointer. Remember, a round pencil will roll off the screen, so use one that is six-sided.

▶ Use the revelation technique to reveal each point on the transparency one at a time. Put a piece of paper under the transparency and slide it down to reveal each point. (If you put it on top of the transparency, the paper will slip off the moment you take your fingers away from it.)

▶ Don't fiddle around with the overhead projector between transparencies. Your movements are distracting to your audience.

▶ Know exactly where the projector's power button is located. Turn the projector's lamp off before you remove the transparency, place the next transparency on the glass, and then turn the lamp on again. That way, you'll avoid blinding your audience with the bright light emitted from an empty overhead projector.

▶ To prolong the life of the projector's bulb and to prevent sudden shattering, run the fan a few minutes after turning off the lamp.

▶ Always have an emergency bulb ready in the event the one in the projector burns out. Often one is stored in a compartment inside the projector itself.

Slides—Photographic and Digital

Millions of projectors and photographic slides are in use in the training and presentation world despite the burgeoning popularity of digital slides, which can be projected directly from a laptop using PowerPoint software. The basic advice for the use of slides, whether they are photographic or digital, is very much the same.

When to Use Slides. Slides certainly are a step up from transparencies. Here are some pointers on when to use slides:

▶ *Your presentation is formal, and you want to present a professional image.* Making slides is not much of a technical issue, especially if you have access to a digital projector and you have minimal expertise with Microsoft's PowerPoint program.

▶ *Your audience is large.* Large venues can support large screen presentations.

▶ *You will be repeating the presentation frequently.* Photographic slides can be archived in protective pages made for three-ring binders, or you can store them right in slide carousels, ready to pop into a projector. You can store a digital slide presentation on floppy discs or burn it onto a CD-RW. It's best to do both so you'll have a backup should you need it.

When Not to Use Slides. Just as one size does not fit all, neither are slides the right audiovisual for all situations, for example:

> ► *Your presentation is informal or not consistent with the atmosphere you are look-ing to establish.* Yes, you may use photographic or digital slides in a small room during an informal presentation, but why go to the trouble when a simple flipchart would be just as effective?
>
> ► *You wish to make changes either before your program or on the fly.* The advantage of a flipchart or an overhead transparency is that you can make changes dur-ing a presentation without opening a computer software program. If you are using traditional slides, revisions can be costly in terms of time and money.

Slide Basics. To make your slides effective and appealing, use contrasting colors that show well to your audience. Use headings and bullet points in slides to separate items.

As is the case with any high-tech audiovisuals, you must know your equipment. If you are using traditional slides, make sure that they are in the slide tray or carousel correctly. Trainers have been embarrassed for years by forgetting this detail only to find that the slides are in upside-down or backward.

Make sure that your audience will be able to see the slides without difficulty. Dim the room lights or draw the shades. Don't make it too dark, though, because audi-ences have been known to fall asleep in such an environment. Don't stand in front of your slides; instead, use a pointer (such as a laser pointer) to emphasize points.

PowerPoint

PowerPoint has taken the presentation world by storm! PowerPoint is a Microsoft software program that has become the visual support of choice for presenters look-ing to leave an impression as well as inform. So popular is PowerPoint that it's a rare organization where someone isn't using it to make a sales presentation to customers or prospective customers, introduce a new product, or simply provide information for employees. All you need is the software to produce the slides and you're set to go. Because PowerPoint comes with Microsoft Office, you may have it already. If not, you can purchase the software separately.

PowerPoint is used to create digital slides that can be shown to your audience in a number of ways including

> ► a tabletop computer or liquid crystal diode (LCD) display on a laptop com-puter for small groups
>
> ► a digital projector that interfaces directly with a laptop or PDA (special accessory required)

- a computer projector that projects images directly from your monitor onto a screen or flat surface for larger groups
- an overhead projector that uses specially made transparencies
- over the Internet or your organization's intranet
- hard copies of your slides that can be distributed as handouts.

PowerPoint offers many advantages over traditional audiovisual aids. One such advantage is that for a tool so advanced technologically, PowerPoint is surprisingly easy to use. For example, the program includes slide templates into which you can insert information and data. Another convenient feature of PowerPoint is the ability to have your notes written on the slide that can be seen by the presenter but not by the audience. All that's needed is a little ingenuity, the right software, and a laptop, and you are ready to give a dynamite presentation.

When to Use PowerPoint. You can use PowerPoint in much the same way you would use slides. Because they are technologically superior, consider using digital slides when:

- *Your presentation is formal.* PowerPoint presentations are impressive not only for the high quality of each image produced but because of the ability you have to add movement, animation, and sound to each slide.
- *You present the same program regularly.* Because your presentation can be saved to a disk, CD-ROM, a laptop, or even a PDA, your presentation is easily stored and transported. This feature means no bulky slide trays or flimsy transparencies to worry about.
- *You need the flexibility to modify your presentation.* PowerPoint allows you to add or replace slides, as well as text and just about anything else you might want to revise with a few strokes on your computer keyboard. An added advantage is that you can make most changes right at the point you need it.
- *You will be giving the same presentation for groups of different sizes.* PowerPoint presentations are just as appropriate for a large group sitting in a conference center as they are for a presentation for one or two people sitting around a conference table. In the first case, you'd probably use a digital projector, and for the second case, you'd just use your laptop or a desktop monitor set on the table.
- *You want to be creative.* You can be as creative as you want with the graphics you are able to use with PowerPoint. You can easily produce anything from

graphs and charts to an animated presentation with sound effects. You can insert clipart, scanned images or documents, or even photos from a digital camera right into your PowerPoint documents. You can capitalize on these features to make your presentations powerful and entertaining.

▶ *You want to use the revelation technique.* You also have the ability to be creative in how each slide is presented. For example, the animation feature of PowerPoint allows you to "build" a slide starting with one line on a slide and, with a click of the remote, add additional lines one by one, eventually showing all the lines together. Even the transition between slides can be made to look like everything from a pair of blinds opening to images that fade in and out.

When Not to Use PowerPoint. With a tool so much more advanced than most traditional audiovisual aids you might wonder if there's ever a time when it's not appropriate to use it. Although PowerPoint is far superior in presentation quality than traditional audiovisual aids, there are some caveats for its use:

▶ *Your presentation needs flexibility.* As an informational or sales tool, PowerPoint is generally unsurpassed as a means of catching people's attention, as well as presenting information and data in myriad creative ways. Usually these presentations are designed to deliver a particular message in a structured way. But, that's not appropriate for all your presentations. For example, in a training presentation, the flexibility to deviate from what has been prepared is often what makes the experience so rich for the audience. Reliance upon the prepared digital slides and accompanying script can lead to a loss of spontaneity that really engages an audience.

▶ *You're somewhat phobic about new technology.* Because some presenters are still fearful of new technology, they can easily find themselves more concerned about pressing the right remote button than giving their presentation. Such issues will disappear the more you use PowerPoint and become comfortable using it. Just remember that the visual should *never* be the message, so don't make the beauty of PowerPoint overtake the purpose of your presentation.

▶ *Your audience has seen a few too many PowerPoint presentations.* Many presenters are jumping on the PowerPoint bandwagon, but audiences can get too much of a good thing. People can grow weary of sitting in darkened rooms watching yet another set of digital slides fading in and out, with bullet points sliding across the screen. Mix things up! Use PowerPoint for some presentations but not for all. Or, use PowerPoint for the formal part of your presentation and a flipchart to take down key points during a facilitated Q & A session.

PowerPoint Basics. Dozens of books have been written about effective use of PowerPoint (chapter 9), but it's easy to get started on your own. The program is very intuitive and the wizards, templates, and tutorials can help you create great-looking presentations in record time. Basically, you have three ways to create a PowerPoint presentation:

1. AutoContent wizard: This feature provides you with a step-by-step guide for developing various types of presentations and is ideal for those who still consider overhead projectors to be high-tech.
2. Templates: These tools provide you with various standard formats, including backgrounds, headers, titles, and bullet points, for creating slides. This approach is ideal for those who are comfortable with the technology but don't want to go through the bother of creating slides from scratch.
3. Creating slides from scratch: Although you can develop your presentation from the ground up, it's not as easy as using the wizards and templates that come with the program. Nevertheless, this approach gives you maximum flexibility.

Because PowerPoint is such a powerful presentation tool, many presenters tend to rely on it as the sole source of audiovisual support for their presentations. But, even PowerPoint can wear thin on an audience. Try incorporating other aids to break things up and keep your audience engaged.

Keep in mind, too, that it's easy to get carried away with all the graphics, animation, and images you can create with PowerPoint, so be careful not to create sensory overload for your audience. As is true for most visual aids, beware of being too wordy when developing your slides. Many accomplished PowerPoint presenters recommend a six-by-six format: six lines per slide, six words per line. Remember the focus should be on the main speaking points and key words.

Because it's so easy to print out the slides, consider, if appropriate, using the copies as handouts. Regardless of whether you distribute copies of your slides to the audience, be sure to bring a hard copy that you can reproduce in case your computer or digital projector crashes. Of course, you'll also need spare floppy discs just in case, as well as backup PowerPoint files on floppy disc and CD-RW. Even better—print a set of transparencies of your PowerPoint slides. Should computer technology break down at your presentation site, you can use the transparencies for your presentation.

Videotapes and DVDs

Using informational videotapes and DVDs can be an effective part of a presentation, as a means of getting across a concept, providing background information, or simply offering some entertainment or a catalyst for discussion. If you think you might want to use a video or DVD, the following are some points to consider.

When to Use Videotape or DVD. Use videotape in your presentation when you want to illustrate a point in a dramatic fashion, or if you wish to entertain as well as inform your audience. These visual aids are particularly effective for demonstrating desired skills and behaviors.

When Not to Use Videotape or DVD. Not all presentations lend themselves to the use of videotape. Do not use a video if:

- *Your time is limited.* Videos are often used to stimulate discussion. The show is not very valuable if you don't have time to discuss the contents.
- *You want to update or change your message.* Changes made to a video are expensive and can be tricky.

Video Basics. As is true for any visual aid, proper presentation and a few techniques can enhance your presentation. Keep these tips in mind:

- Make sure you have the proper equipment, that it works, and that you know how to use it. Nothing is more embarrassing than apologizing for equipment mix-ups or your own lack of expertise.
- Depending on the size of the room and audience, make sure that there are enough monitors throughout the room so that the entire audience can see. Usually a minimum of a 25-inch monitor strategically placed will do the trick. Once again, don't get caught looking unprepared by having a single monitor sitting on a table in the front of the room and 50 people craning their necks to see the great videotape you brought in.

▶ Show short segments of video to make points; in some cases don't play the video more than 10–15 minutes without a break to discuss it.

▶ When you purchase a training video/DVD, you automatically have permission to use that video in your presentations as you see fit. However, commercial videos/DVDs do not fall into this category. If you purchase or rent a popular movie and use it in a presentation without written permission from the film producers, it is a possible violation of copyright law, depending on the nature of your use and the organization in which the presentation takes place. Check this out before making a commercial movie part of your presentation.

Visual Props

Often overlooked as visual aids that you can use during your presentation are props. Only your imagination limits the types of props that you can use. For example, one presenter took a basketball in one hand and a baseball in the other as he described the difference in weight of two issues he was presenting. Still another creative presenter handed out dollars as a reward each time someone in the audience answered a question correctly. (If you try this approach, make sure you ask only tough questions!)

Introducing anything like props into your presentation takes a little courage. After all, the approach might not fly, or people might not quite understand the symbolism. Try out your props when you are doing a run-through of your presentation with friends or colleagues. Who knows, you might just find that your attempt at creativity is what makes your presentation special in their eyes.

Handouts

A different kind of visual aid is what are commonly referred to as handouts. Handouts usually consist of either additional information related to your presentation or are the hard copies of what was presented on a visual such as a flipchart or transparency. Handouts are important for a number of reasons:

▶ They reinforce any and all learning from the presentation.

▶ They free up people to listen to what you are presenting rather than taking lots of notes.

▶ They allow you to provide information to your audience beyond what you covered in your presentation.

▶ They allow your audience to personalize the materials by taking notes or highlighting important information as the presentation progresses.

It is usually wise to provide handouts for your presentation, whenever appropriate, and to give the handouts to your audience after the presentation rather than before. Perhaps you have a logical reason for delivering handouts before the presentation (for example, to encourage your audience to take notes during the presentation), but if the audience has the handouts beforehand they are more likely to pay attention to the handouts than to you. No presenter likes to stand there talking while their audience is sifting through pages of a handout. Another reason to provide handouts after your presentation is to add a little suspense to your presentation, rather than revealing up front what you plan on covering.

If you decide to provide handouts before your presentation, have them already laid out, whenever possible, on the tables or chairs where your audience will be seated. If you plan to hand them out after your presentation, make arrangements ahead of time to have someone assist you, especially if your audience is a large one. It's a little tacky to be speaking to your audience, wrapping up your presentation, and be delivering handouts all at the same time.

Here's the deal on handouts. If you are going to use handouts, you need to look at them in the same way as your other visuals, in terms of being of professional quality. You don't necessarily have to pay someone to design, create, and print your handouts, but the handouts must have a consistent and professional look. If you're using computer-generated visuals, your handouts will probably look fine because what you'll be delivering are hard copies of what you are showing.

Be careful also of using too many different styles and fonts. Definitely make sure that all your copies have a nice, clean look with no misspellings. Remember you wouldn't show a series of transparencies that had an inconsistent format, so the same principle applies to your handouts. And, don't ever get caught without enough handouts. If you are anticipating 20 people in attendance, make and bring a few extra copies just in case. Consider stapling the handouts together or attaching them with a paper clip if they are all being handed out at the same time. For special occasions, you can put the handouts in a folder to keep them together. If you know that they are to be stored in a three-ring binder, your audience will appreciate it if the hole-punching has been done already.

Microphones

Microphones are wonderful inventions that allow audiences at sales meetings and Broadway musicals alike to hear presentations. Though microphones are nearly ubiquitous now, plenty of presenters still make mistakes that cost time and cause embarrassment. Read on for more information about the three main types of microphones you're likely to encounter as a presenter.

Handheld Microphones. Most handheld microphones these days are wireless, but you still run across some that are attached to an amplifier via a long, cumbersome cord that can make you feel anchored to your stage. Here are some tips on using handheld microphones:

- ▶ Don't forget that you have a microphone. Every sound, whether it's a whispered remark to a colleague, a cough, or an accidental bump against the lectern, is heard by the audience.
- ▶ Test the sensitivity of the microphone—before your audience arrives! No one likes to be subjected to the presenter repeating, "Testing 1-2-3." Find the right distance between your mouth and the microphone to avoid feedback and ensure that your audience can hear you.
- ▶ Try to be natural holding the microphone and think of it as an extension of your hand.

Lavaliere Microphones. A lavaliere microphone clips to your lapel, blouse, or pocket with the transmission unit in your pocket or attached to your belt. It allows you to walk around and speak in a natural manner. Most are wireless, but again, you may run across microphones that are still attached by a cord. Here are some pointers for use of lavaliere microphones:

- ▶ Make sure the microphone is in a position to pick up your voice before your presentation.
- ▶ Turn your microphone's transmission unit off when you're not using it. Again, noise and perhaps embarrassing comments might be heard by the audience.

Noted

Even if you have a booming voice that everyone can probably hear, use a microphone if it is handy. A filled room has different acoustics than an empty room.

Podium Microphone. Microphones attached to podiums are still very common. You are trapped behind the podium, which bothers some presenters,

Table 6-1. A matrix to help you make the right choice of audiovisuals.

Audiovisual Type	When to Use	Advantages	Disadvantages
Flipchart and Easel	• Informal presentation • Small number of participants • Small room size • Last-minute presentation • Low budget	• Inexpensive • Quick to set up • Easy to produce • Easy to use • Use on the fly • Readily modified	• Not good for larger audiences • Not good for large rooms • Not good for those with bad handwriting • Not long lasting
Overhead Transparencies	• Informal or formal presentations • Small or large rooms • Low budget	• Relatively inexpensive • Quick to set up • Easy to produce • Easy to use • Long lasting • Use on the fly	• Room too small for projector • Less formal than slides • Need specific equipment
Slides	• Formal presentations • Small or large rooms • Repeating presentations • Looking to impress	• Looks professional • Long lasting • Captures attention	• Relatively expensive • Not that easy to produce • Not easy to change • Need specific equipment
PowerPoint	• Formal presentation • Small or large room • Looking to entertain • Looking to impress • Repeating presentation	• Looks professional • Long lasting • Captures attention • Easily modified before or after presentation • Wide range of formats	• Expenses for software, computer, and projection equipment • Need specific equipment • Need specific training to use • Limited flexibility to modify while in use • Perceived as too technical
Videotape/DVD	• Informal or formal presentation • Small or large rooms • Looking to entertain • Looking to impress • Repeating presentation	• Looks professional • Long lasting • Captures attention	• Expensive • Not easy to produce • Not easy to change • Need specific equipment • Limited time

Table 6-1. A matrix to help you make the right choice of audiovisuals (continued).

Audiovisual Type	When to Use	Advantages	Disadvantages
Visual Props	• Make a visual representation • Capture attention	• Readily remembered • Usually inexpensive • Easy to produce	• Presents some risks • Not everyone understands symbolism
Handouts	• Provide hard copies of visuals • Provide additional information	• Frees up audience to listen rather than take notes • Provides additional information • Inexpensive • Easy to produce	• Distracting if distributed before presentation
Handheld Microphone	• To project voice	• Need flexibility to move around	• Cumbersome • Tendency to move away from mouth • Another thing to take care of • Subject to movement
Lavaliere Microphone	• To project voice	• Need flexibility to move around • No worries about holding or dropping • Unobtrusive	• May forget you have on • May require help in putting on and taking off • Subject to movement
Attached Microphone	• To project voice	• No worries about holding • Not subject to movement • Often accompanied by light • Often attached to lectern	• Restricts movement • Too easy to latch on to • Too easy to fall back on reading directly from notes

but, on the other hand, it does provide novice presenters with some security. Here are some pointers for podium microphones:

▶ Don't cling to the podium with a death grip.

▶ Don't read from your notes just because they're right there in front of you on the podium.

▶ Even if you can't move around, you can still use nonverbal communication to connect with your audience.

Basic Rule 18

No one looks more foolish to an audience than a presenter who doesn't know how to use his or her audiovisual equipment. Know what you're doing before you make your presentation.

Getting It Done

Exercise 6-1 will allow you to not only revisit the major points in this chapter, but you will also have the opportunity to hone your newly learned skills and actually apply them to help you effectively use audiovisual aids to support your presentation.

Exercise 6-1. Using audiovisuals to support your presentation.

1. I've assessed my presentation and know which audiovisuals to use. Yes_____ No_____.
    Jot down some notes here:

    _____

    _____

2. I know how to use the audiovisuals and necessary equipment, and I've done sufficient practice. Yes_____ No_____. Jot down some notes here:

    _____

    _____

3. I've determined that the room can accommodate my audiovisual selection.
    Yes_____ No_____. Jot down some notes here:

    _____

    _____

4. I've prepared my audiovisuals and am ready to go. Yes_____ No_____. Jot down some
    notes here:

    _____

    _____

5. I've arranged for the audiovisual equipment to be shipped (if necessary) and set up in the
    room at the site of my presentation. Yes_____ No_____. Jot down some notes here:

    _____

    _____

6. I know whom to contact in the event I have a problem with my audiovisuals.
    Yes_____ No_____. Jot down some notes here:

    _____

    _____

7. I have considered other important factors such as the following:
    ☐ Room size
    ☐ Group size
    ☐ Lighting and window coverings
    ☐ Nature of presentation
    ☐ Time available
    ☐ My audience's wants and needs

Problems can happen despite all your planning and preparation. In chapter 7 you will learn how to prevent problems from occurring and what to do when things go wrong.

7

When Things Go Wrong

■ ■

 What's Inside This Chapter

Here, you'll see how to:
- ▶ Develop a recovery plan to ensure your presentation's success despite any challenge that may arise
- ▶ Prepare a presenter's toolkit to deal with just about any presentation problem
- ▶ Check out a room to prevent problems before your presentation
- ▶ Handle logistical problems before they get out of hand
- ▶ Deal with audiovisual challenges
- ▶ Manage issues related to your audience
- ▶ Recover when you've lost your place or drawn a blank

This book has focused thus far on two key components for becoming a successful presenter: professionalism and preparation. Even presenters who are professional, prepared, credible, and trustworthy face potentially embarrassing disasters at some point. The main difference between you and these more seasoned presenters is that experienced presenters are better prepared for the times when things go wrong.

This chapter will help you develop a recovery plan to face these inevitable situations in a professional manner. No author can promise a complete sourcebook to address every situation you might face, and, frankly, the common sense that you already have will carry you through most situations. What you'll find here are some of the most common problems you might face and some ways to solve them.

Basic Rule 19

You can prevent many problems if you anticipate before your presentation what can go wrong and take care of potential problems then.

Developing a Recovery Plan

Obviously you can't plan for every possible situation you might face when you're standing in front of a crowd of people. Nevertheless, an ounce of prevention is worth a pound of cure. The following list of a dozen critical steps will help you think about and create your own recovery plan to implement in case things don't go quite right. If you develop and memorize your recovery plan, you'll be able to act quickly to prevent embarrassment and maintain your professional demeanor no matter what happens!

1. As soon as you know you will be making a presentation, contact the individuals who will have an effect on the success of your presentation. These may include the sponsor, audiovisual coordinator, hotel or conference representative, caterer, housekeeper, and any others you can think of. Discuss what you will need and find out if any limitations will be imposed on your presentation.
2. The night before your presentation, review all the materials you'll be using, especially any visuals, to make sure everything is in order and ready to be used.

Basic Rule 20

If you make a habit of bringing extra markers, masking tape, scissors, and the like in your presenter's toolkit, you'll never have to worry about having to rely on others when you have a need.

3. Always have at your side your presenter's toolkit to use in the event of a problem or in case an item is not available on site. Table 7-1 lists some of the items you may wish to include in your toolkit, depending on the type of presentation you're doing and the level of technology you're using.

4. Prior to your presentation, check with the program coordinator, the audio-visual expert, or others who helped you get ready for your presentation to ensure that they have fulfilled their supporting roles. Making friends could be a key factor in your success if something goes wrong.

5. If you are presenting off site, ship your presentation materials so that they'll arrive at least two days before your presentation to make sure you have some leeway if the shipment is delayed. Use the shipper's tracking service to make sure your materials arrive on time. Don't assume anything!

6. Arrive at your presentation location at least 15 minutes prior to your presentation even if you are familiar with the location. Give yourself at least 30 minutes if your presentation is off site or at an unfamiliar location to ensure that the room is set up properly and all equipment and materials are ready to go.

7. After you have settled into your presentation location, check to make sure any audiovisual equipment you plan to use is in working order and that you are familiar with its operation.

Table 7-1. Some items to consider keeping in your presenter's toolkit.

☐ Business cards	☐ Masking tape
☐ Clear tape	☐ Nontoxic, water-soluble markers
☐ Correction fluid	☐ Paper
☐ Duct tape or gaff tape for extension cord safety	☐ Paperclips
	☐ Pencil sharpener
☐ Erasers	☐ Pens and sharpened pencils
☐ Extension cord and power strip	☐ Post-it notes
☐ Floppy disks and/or blank CD-ROMs	☐ Projector bulbs
☐ Grease pencil or transparency markers	☐ Rubber bands
☐ Highlighter	☐ Scissors
☐ Hole punch	☐ Stapler and staple remover
☐ Index cards (especially the kind you prepared your notes on)	☐ Staples
	☐ Tape measure and ruler
☐ Laser pointer	☐ Transparencies

8. Do a quick check of the room. Note where the light switches are located and that they function properly. Check to make sure that your audience will be able to see you and any audiovisuals you plan to use. Check for loose cords or any other possible hazards to your audience and you. Make sure your microphone works and if possible do a sound check by asking someone to stand at the back of the room to ensure you will be heard by everyone in the audience.

9. Look at yourself in a mirror. Are you looking good?

10. If possible, greet your audience members as they arrive. This little gesture boosts your credibility and helps your audience have a better impression of you.

11. Run through the checklist in figure 7-1 to be sure you've covered all the bases. You can print out the checklist and keep it in your toolkit, or you could even load it into your PDA.

12. Take a deep breath, say to yourself, "I'm prepared, and I am going to do great!" Relax, smile, and have a good time.

Figure 7-1. A last-minute checklist.

☐ Do a last-minute review of your notes and fine-tune your presentation.

☐ Do a run-through of your presentation with a friend or colleague observing, listening, and providing feedback.

☐ Check to make sure you have the proper date, time, and location for your presentation.

☐ Gather together any materials you will be using, ensuring they are ready to go.

☐ Review all visuals to make sure all is in order and all words are spelled properly.

☐ If you are using any presentation technology, be it an overhead projector or a laptop computer, make sure it works—and that you know how to work it.

☐ Check with your sponsor, contact person, audiovisual expert, or other support staff to ensure that all logistical and audiovisual arrangements have been made.

☐ Double-check your presenter's toolkit (table 7-1), and replenish supplies as needed.

☐ Prepare yourself mentally by envisioning a successful presentation in your mind.

☐ Use positive self-talk to build your confidence. Say to yourself, "I'm prepared, and I'll do great!"

☐ Get a good night's sleep.

Logistical Nightmares
Right Room, Wrong Setup

One reason for arriving early is to give you a little time to fix a room that has been improperly set up. Despite all your preparation, if you do much presenting, this scenario *will* happen no matter how well you plan and follow up.

First, don't panic. Although room setup is important, focus first on any glaring issues the setup presents. For example, will your audience be able to see and hear you (including your visuals) from every corner of the room? If the wrong setup does not present any major issues for your presentation, adapt to the situation, make a few minor adjustments, and count yourself lucky. If the setup is a problem, stay calm, contact the proper authority, and explain clearly what you need to have done. If you followed the advice to make friends with those responsible for setting up your room (step 4), then you'll be in a better position to fix the problem because you know who to call and they know you.

Don't waste your time and energy blaming people at this point. Graciously thank those whom you recruited to make adjustments, and leave any discussion about the room setup until after your presentation. But remember this: *Don't settle for a room that will prevent you from presenting the information that your audience needs. It's your presentation and your reputation that are on the line.*

External Noise

How many times have you been sitting in a presentation trying to hear the presenter over the clattering in a nearby dining room, the pounding of a jackhammer at a nearby construction site, or the droning of a speech from an adjacent room? The bottom line is simply that you should not have to endure this distraction and neither should your audience.

Depending on when the offending noise is noticed, it's perfectly acceptable to ask for a different room or maybe even handle the situation yourself by closing doors. Again, don't put yourself in a position where you won't be at your very best. You're in charge, and "I'm sorry" is a pretty weak excuse for most in your audience who are suffering along with you.

A Large Room and Few Attendees

If only a few people show up for your presentation, don't take it personally. Somebody probably dropped the ball when it came to publicity. First, try a little humor to coax those sitting in the far reaches of the room to come forward, perhaps something like: "You look a little lonely out there, would you mind sitting a little closer to the front? I promise not to embarrass anyone in the front row." It usually works. As people comply, remember the power of a thank you. Humor can build rapport with your audience and make your audience comfortable and accepting of what you have to say. Taking a schoolmarmish approach by asking all the attendees to move to the front won't help you deal with this situation.

Audiovisual Equipment Snafus

Yes, you thought you had considered everything and you were assured all was in order, but slip-ups happen. Again, your preparation may pay dividends because you should know whom to contact for help. If you've already made the acquaintance of the audiovisual expert (step 4 of your recovery plan), try to get in touch with him or her right away. Again, early arrival is the key to being on top of this situation. But, what if the equipment you wanted—a slide projector, for example—just isn't available or doesn't work?

Go back to the basics; think flipchart! Sometimes low-tech is the only solution available that will permit the show to go on. Since you were prepared for what might go wrong, you should have paper copies of the slides—photographic or digital—you intended to use. Ask for a flipchart and easel (most locations have both), and write out the important points of what you were going to present. To make things a little easier for you, write in light pencil on the edges of your flipchart some notes to help you get through this mini-crisis. If you had planned to give your audience a paper copy of your visuals, you're in even better shape. Explain the situation and ask your audience to follow along using their paper copies.

Another option for larger audiences may be to convert your digital or photographic slides to overheads (assuming that an overhead projector is available). Take your paper copies and have them photocopied onto transparencies. You should have spare transparencies in your toolkit (see table 7-1). You're all set!

Here are some tips on how to talk your way gracefully out of this situation:

▶ Use humor. It works in most sticky situations like this. Explain what happened and put on your best song and dance routine. The audience will probably cut you a break if you handle the situation correctly.

▶ If you have paper copies of your presentation, pass them out. Web technology comes in handy here. Promise to put your visuals on a Website, available for download.

▶ Go ahead and make your presentation with confidence. You'll impress your audience with your ability to think on your feet.

Projector Lamp Burnout. Another common equipment problem is bulb failure in slide or overhead projectors. If, as part of your preparation, you asked for one to be available then you're set.

You may either change the bulb yourself, or you may ask for a 10-minute break to contact your audiovisual friend and have this person fix it. Again, humor is the best medicine for this situation: "Have you ever had a day when you think things can't get any worse and then . . . ?" Most audiences are forgiving when something like this happens, especially if you are prepared to deal with it. If it cannot be fixed in a timely manner, remember the flipchart fallback.

Misspelled Words and Other Problems. Depending on the technology you are using, the fix can be as simple as a few keystrokes on your laptop computer to fix a PowerPoint slide beamed directly from your computer through a digital projector. If you are going low-tech, then you'll have what you need in your toolkit.

With correction fluid, scissors, clear tape, and markers, you can make a quick fix on your flipchart with a cut-and-paste job. If you have to re-create a flipchart page, you can use the blank one you should have left between the sheets of your flipchart pad (chapter 6).

Wrong Flipchart Holder/Easel. Not all flipchart holders are created equal. If you happen to get the wrong type for your flipchart and the proper one is not available, try to find a wire coat hanger and rig up a quick fix. Necessity is the mother of invention, right?

Dropping Your Transparencies. Don't get flustered. Your audience will pick up on your tension, only making the problem worse. If you numbered your transparencies, you'll be in pretty good shape. As you bend down to pick them up, try a little humor delivered with a smile: "I always wondered what would happen if I dropped all my transparencies, and now I know. If you'll bear with me, I'll put these back in order and we'll be ready to go."

Audience Challenges

Disruptive Audience Members. In most instances realize that most of the audience is on your side and would like for the disruption to stop. On the other hand, the audience is waiting to see how you'll handle the situation. If you get angry you have lost control of the situation, and your credibility suffers.

The most unobtrusive way of dealing with inappropriate behavior by an audience member is to look at him or her directly eye to eye for three to five seconds. This is a nonverbal way of saying, "Cut it out!" If this approach doesn't work, calmly ask if the person has a question or comment. Third-grade teachers handle disruptive children this way, and it usually works for adults, too. If the disruption continues, call for a brief break and speak to the disruptive person directly.

The Eager Beaver Questioner. Questions are good because they usually show interest if not always agreement. There are times, however, when an individual in your audience monopolizes the session. Here are some ways to deal with these folks:

- ▸ Acknowledge the audience member's interest and explain that you'd like to answer all questions, but time does not permit. Then move on.
- ▸ Explain that you would appreciate questions at the end of your presentation.
- ▸ Offer to stay after the presentation to answer questions.

Dead Silence. What if no one has any questions? It can definitely be an awkward moment if you invite questions and then the room becomes so quiet that you could hear a pin drop. This situation is especially challenging if you have set aside 15 minutes at the end of your presentation for questions. It just might be that you covered the topic so effectively that no one has any questions that were not addressed by your presentation.

If the audience initially feels overwhelmed with new information, they may need some time, perhaps over a break, to formulate questions. In some cases, you may be able to provide an email address or other means for the audience to contact you after the presentation with questions.

If no one has a question, it's perfectly reasonable to turn the tables and ask the audience a question relating to your presentation. You might even say, "Because no one seems to have any questions now, I have a question for you." Then ask the audience one or a series of questions until you get a response. Often, one response leads to another and pretty soon you have a discussion going.

Strong Disagreement to Your Presentation. Sometimes an audience member strongly disagrees with the material or point of view you have presented. Here are some ways you can try to defuse this disagreement:

▶ Remind yourself that everyone is entitled to an opinion, so don't get angry or hurt, and don't take it personally.

▶ If you think the disagreement is becoming personal, steer the conversation back to the subject under discussion. Remember the presentation is about your subject, not about you. This realization should help alleviate the temptation to defend yourself, which lessens your credibility and is ultimately a no-win situation.

▶ Acknowledge the other person's point of view and be respectful of his or her opinions, without agreeing to something you disagree with. You can also use your facilitation skills, if time allows, to encourage others in the audience to express their thoughts on the subject.

▶ Finally, remind yourself that this is still your presentation and that you have control. There may come a point where you'll have to exercise the power of the presenter and very professionally and courteously move on.

Where Is Everybody? Waiting for your audience to show up can be a stress-inducing time. You're all ready to go, you have a little adrenaline surge, but many of the chairs are still empty. If you wait too long or if you don't wait long enough for a full audience, you risk your credibility.

It's frustrating to present to a half-empty room or being interrupted by latecomers, but waiting too long frustrates those who did arrive on time. It's your call and it is situational, but the consequences of making the wrong decision can mean the difference between a successful presentation and an unsuccessful one.

Forgetting Your Lines

Inexperienced actors and first-time presenters share the fear of flubbing their lines. You think, "What if I can't remember (even with my notes) what I'm supposed to say or do?" Again, if you are prepared and follow the simple recommendations in this book, you won't face this situation. Sometimes, though, you may lose your line of thought if someone interrupts with a question, if a projector lamp burns out, or if you drop your transparencies.

Noted

Making the wrong decision about whether to wait for late arrivals can really damage your credibility with those who arrived on time. Still you need to walk a fine line between sticking to the schedule and meeting the needs of everyone in your audience. Every situation is different, so good judgment is the key. Ask for your sponsor's (if available) input on the decision about when to begin. If you cannot get your sponsor's input, consider waiting up to 10 minutes or so, and then say something like this: "We're still waiting for some additional people to arrive. If it's all right with the group, I'd like to start now and as people arrive I'll do my best to get them caught up with what I'm presenting." Unless someone in the audience objects, stick with your decision and move forward.

To get back on track, try this approach: Acknowledge to your audience, if appropriate, that you've lost your train of thought. Light humor can lessen the anxiety for both you and your audience. You might say, "Has it ever happened to you that you suddenly lose your train of thought? Just give me a second, and I'll find my place and we'll be ready to go." Consult your notes to determine where you left off and pick up from there. Remember, most audiences will forgive you as long as you remain cool and confident.

Final Tips

This chapter has covered only some of the things that can go wrong with your presentation. As you have seen, being prepared and remaining professional are the two most important ingredients in handling any issue that may arise. Here are nine more tips you should remember to get past these potentially embarrassing presentation problems:

1. Make sure you know the appropriate dress for your presentation. Nothing is more embarrassing than being over- or underdressed, and you're the person everyone is looking at.
2. Don't pass up the opportunity, especially when asked, to express your requirements for your presentation. For example, if you believe your presentation would work best in a small, intimate room with a flipchart

Basic Rule 21
When things go wrong, keep cool! If you maintain a professional demeanor as you overcome problems, the more forgiving and accepting your audience will be.

and easel, then it's important to say so. Do whatever you can to help make yourself a successful presenter!

3. Write out your own introduction because it's often the first bit of information that your audience will receive about you. See to it that your audience learns what you would like them to know about yourself.

4. If food will be served during your presentation, decide when it will be delivered to lessen the interruption. Remember, food inside makes for easy access but more noise and distractions; if the food service is set up outside your room, it leaves the possibility that people may miss parts of your presentation, although there's less noise and distraction.

5. If you need help distributing materials or hanging flipchart pages around the room, enlist those individuals prior to the program and carefully explain what you need them to do and when.

6. When appropriate, make friends in the room by greeting people as they walk in the room. The more support you enlist, the better.

7. Find out before your presentation where the lavatories are. Determine whether it is appropriate to give this information out to your audience prior to your presentation.

8. Resist the temptation to make any significant changes in your presentation right before you are ready to start. It is one thing to fine-tune; but changes in your presentation may have a ripple effect on other parts of it that you might not have thought through.

9. Get off to a good start by having down pat the first 60–90 seconds of your presentation. If you start out on the right foot, the rest will be a piece of cake!

Getting It Done

This chapter has provided you with a sampling of the many things that can (and will) go wrong if you make enough presentations. Old pros have many war stories involving the situations mentioned in this chapter and many other situations that you probably wouldn't even believe could happen. Nevertheless, with your solid preparation, prework, and your presenter's toolkit, you can prevent many potential problems or solve them quickly and professionally while winning the audience over to your side.

Exercise 7-1 can help you commit to memory the recovery plan offered in this chapter. After all, when you face a last-minute problem, you don't want to fumble through books or other materials to figure out what to do.

Exercise 7-1. Developing a recovery plan to implement in the event of a last-minute problem.

1. I have contacted everyone who has a stake in my presentation, and we are all clear about how they will support me. Yes_____ No_____. Jot down some notes here:

   _____

   _____

   _____

2. I have my presenter's toolkit well stocked and ready to go. Yes_____ No_____. Jot down some notes here:

   _____

   _____

   _____

3. I have arranged for any materials, as well as my audiovisual equipment to be delivered and set up. Yes_____ No_____. Jot down some notes here:

   _____

   _____

   _____

4. I have checked the presentation room to ensure that it meets my specifications. Yes_____ No_____. Jot down some notes here:

   _____

   _____

   _____

5. I am confident about using all my audiovisual aids. Yes_____ No_____. Jot down some notes here:

   _____

   _____

   _____

6. I have anticipated and am prepared to meet any challenges from my audience.
    Yes_____ No_____. Jot down some notes here:

    _____

    _____

    _____

7. I have the first 60-90 seconds of my presentation down pat and I am ready to go.
    Yes_____ No_____. Jot down some notes here:

    _____

    _____

    _____

    _____

Now that you've learned the basics for making an effective presentation, it's important to pursue a path of continuous learning. In chapter 8 you'll begin to do just that as you are introduced to 20 different ways of improving your presentation skills.

8

Improving Your Skills

■■■■■■■■■■■■■■■■■■■■■■■■■■■■■■■■■■■■■■

What's Inside This Chapter

Here, you'll see how to:

▶ Use a variety of experiences—inside and outside the
workplace—to improve your presentation skills
▶ Turn volunteer and community activities into opportunities
for growth as a presenter
▶ Take the next step toward becoming a great presenter

What you've learned in this book are the basics—a jumping-off point for big-
ger and better presentations that you will make in the future. You may not
be a professional presenter, but you are a professional. There's much to learn, but
the exciting part is that learning to present can be a fun and sometimes even exhil-
arating experience. The following 20 actions are suggested to help you grow and
develop as a presenter. Try the ones that suit your needs.

Join Toastmasters

Toastmasters is an organization that helps members to improve their public speaking
skills and gain leadership skills in a supportive environment. At meetings held
throughout the country, individuals have the opportunity to make presentations to

other members and receive feedback. For new presenters (and experienced ones too), joining a Toastmasters group is an excellent investment in their professional development as speakers.

Take a Communications Course

Most colleges and many adult schools offer classes that teach effective presentation skills. Because they always mix practice with theory, they are an excellent way to improve your skill level and get feedback from both a professional (the instructor) and colleagues.

Join a Professional or Social Organization

The point here is to not only join an organization, but also to take advantage of opportunities to share your knowledge with others by presenting to other members on topics of interest. This is an excellent way to hone your skills and, at the same time, build a reputation in your field.

Teach a Class

Nothing is more closely related to giving a presentation, than teaching a class on a subject you are knowledgeable about. In many ways the dynamics of preparation, delivery, and meeting group needs are much the same. Look for opportunities to teach a class at a local community college, adult or night school, or even a class teaching children how to improve their reading at your town's library. Take advantage of any opportunity to stand (or sit) before a group and communicate a message or impart knowledge.

Write an Article

As you have gathered from reading this book, before you stand up and deliver, it's important to write down the points you wish to make in a coherent and easily understood way. That's why any chance to practice your writing skills is well worth taking advantage of. Look for opportunities to write for your company's internal newsletter, local newspaper, professional association journal; or even just short stories for your family and friends.

Become a Volunteer

You might ask what does volunteering have to do with giving a presentation? Most volunteer groups ask members to solicit donations or to encourage others to join through communicating on a one-on-one basis and sometimes through group presentations. What better way to practice your presentation skills and make a difference for a cause you believe in?

Videotape Yourself

Seeing is believing, and nothing helps a new presenter improve his or her performance before a group than watching him- or herself perform on tape. Because most people have access to a videocamera, this makes for an easy and inexpensive way to practice. Videotape a practice run, and then review it with a trusted friend or colleague who can critique your performance. If no videocamera is available, you can get a sense of how you sound to a group by audiotaping a dry run and listening to the playback.

Read Books and Articles

Many excellent books and articles have been written on the subject of how to give a presentation. These are great resources for learning your craft as a presenter. Chapter 9 of this book is an extensive, though not exhaustive, list of publications that you can start with.

Take a Class

A great way to get a leg up on the latest computer-generated visual aid is to take a class on the software. If you haven't already learned how to develop and present a PowerPoint presentation, for example, maybe now is the time to do so. Although PowerPoint isn't the right approach for every presentation you do, this technically advanced means of visual support will not only dazzle your audience, but put you in a category of being up on the latest in presentation visual aids. Many night schools offer programs, but chances are you can get a very thorough education in the use of these tools from your audiovisual coordinator at your organization, through an online course, or a purchased tutorial program.

Observe a Seasoned Pro

Skim your newspaper to see when the next lecture series is playing at your local college or community organization, go to your chapter's professional organization meeting, or simply ask your in-house training guru if you can sit in on a presentation he or she will be making in the future. You'll learn a lot from watching and, if you ask, can probably pick up some excellent professional tips for improvement.

Watch Famous (and Infamous) Presentations

Classic speeches have been archived on videotape and DVD. Your local library no doubt has videos depicting famous presentations by President John F. Kennedy and Reverend Martin Luther King. When you watch these moments closely, you can pick up on the powerful skills of great presenters.

You can also get some helpful tips by watching television talk show hosts and newscasters who earn their keep by making presentations to their viewing audiences. You can see some fine examples of microphone handling; ways to engage an audience; and nonverbal, as well as verbal, communication.

Work on a Committee

Try finding a team, committee, or taskforce either at work or in your community in which the duties involve making presentations. Often these groups issue reports that must be presented to larger bodies and offer excellent opportunities for the beginner presenter to work on both preparation and delivery skills.

Write a Program or Workshop

Perhaps you have a passion for a subject you wish to share, or maybe you've been asked by your organization to prepare and offer a training program. These opportunities give you the chance to show leadership by providing the means for others to take an action or learn something new. Use the steps covered in this book to develop and prepare your presentation and then to take the next big step in delivering a winning presentation.

Attend a Networking Event

You may be asking what does networking have to do with presenting? For starters, both are about communicating with others and both place a premium on being prepared and professional. Networking events are like mini-presentations except that you are usually speaking one-on-one or in small groups. Who knows, you may even meet someone so impressed with you that he or she asks you to come and give a presentation to his or her group.

Practice Your Listening Skills

A networking event is also a good place to practice listening. Take time to practice listening to others. It's a skill that few of us have thoroughly developed so take advantage of every opportunity to practice. As you read in this book, giving a presentation isn't just standing in front of a room of people and talking to them. It's about your audience's needs; the best way to find out what those needs are is to listen.

Join a Theater Group

A fun thing to do is to join a theater group and take a part in a play. You'll be surprised at just how closely related giving a presentation and acting in a play is. If nothing else, acting in a play will help you conquer any nervousness you might have about appearing before a group.

Run a Meeting

Volunteering to facilitate your organization's next meeting is an excellent way of practicing your facilitation skills. That way, you'll be in charge and have to think on your feet (or while sitting down). Good meeting facilitators ask good questions and set an atmosphere where people can interact with and learn from one another.

Hunt for a Job Whether You Need One or Not

Writing a résumé is a great confidence builder, especially one that focuses on your accomplishments. One of the keys to becoming a successful presenter is to feel and look confident. As some of you know, writing a résumé can be tedious work that calls for discipline—the kind of discipline it takes to write a presentation. If you are actually looking for a new position, go on as many interviews as possible. An interview is really a presentation all about you.

Do a Team Presentation

One way to participate in more presentations is to find as many opportunities as you can to present as part of a team or with another colleague. These situations tend to take some of the pressure off because you aren't up there alone.

Set a Goal

Now that you've read this book, it's important to put into action what you've learned. The next logical step in your progression is to give a presentation. Remember: Practice truly does make perfect when it comes to becoming a polished presenter. So choose a topic, set a date, prepare, and just do it!

Getting It Done

Now, how can you apply the ideas in this chapter to improve your presentation skills? Exercise 8-1 offers you the chance to identify your opportunities for growth as a presenter. It is a checklist of the 20 ideas presented in this chapter. Next to each, indicate with a checkmark if the idea might apply to you. Write down some specific notes about how you can follow up on these ideas.

Exercise 8-1. Honing your presentation skills.

☐ Join Toastmasters _____

☐ Take a communications course_____

☐ Join a professional or social organization _____

☐ Teach a class_____

☐ Write an article_____

☐ Become a volunteer _____

☐ Videotape yourself _____

☐ Read books and articles _____

☐ Take a class_____

☐ Observe a seasoned pro _____

☐ Watch famous (and infamous) presentations _____

☐ Work on a committee_____

☐ Write a program or workshop _____

☐ Attend a networking event _____

☐ Practice your listening skills_____

☐ Join a theater group_____

☐ Run a meeting _____

☐ Hunt for a job whether you need one or not _____

☐ Do a team presentation_____

☐ Set a goal _____

The next chapter highlights some specific resources that can help you improve your presentation skills.

9

Where to Get
More Information

■ ■

What's Inside This Chapter

Here, you'll see how to:

▶ Locate resources to give you other viewpoints on presentation basics

▶ Learn more about audiovisual aids

▶ Discover ways to make your presentations fun and engaging for your audiences

▶ Find more information about advanced presentation techniques

*P*resentation Basics is only the beginning of your journey as a presenter. This chapter offers a grab bag of resources to help you develop further as a presenter. Who knows? You may find that making presentations is a real personal strength for you.

Presentation has become a big business, with dozens of books, seminars, audio- and videotapes, and even conferences dedicated to the craft. Just a sampler of the myriad resources available to you is presented here. The chapter is divided into categories to help you quickly locate the information you need. Pick your favorite online bookstore or go to your local bookstore to find many of these resources. Good luck!

Presentation Basics

Arredondo, Lani. *Communicating Effectively.* McGraw-Hill Trade, 2000.

Asher, Spring, and Wicke Chambers. *Wooing & Winning Business: The Foolproof Formula for Making Persuasive Business Presentations.* John Wiley & Sons, 1998.

Bailey, Edward P., Jr., and Larry Bailey. *Plain English at Work: A Guide to Writing and Speaking.* Oxford University Press, 1996.

Barlow, Bob. *Oral Presentations Made Easy!* Scholastic, 2002.

Becker, Dennis, and Paula Borkum Becker. *Powerful Presentation Skills.* McGraw-Hill Trade, 1993.

Berkley, Susan. *Speak to Influence: How to Unlock the Hidden Power of Your Voice.* Campbell Hall Press, 1999.

Bienvenu, Sherron. *The Presentation Skills Workshop: Helping People Create and Deliver Great Presentations (The Trainer's Workshop Series).* AMACOM, 1999.

Booher, Dianna. *Communicate With Confidence!* McGraw-Hill Trade, 1994.

Booher, Dianna. *Speak With Confidence: Powerful Presentations That Inform, Inspire and Persuade.* McGraw-Hill Trade, 2002.

Bowman, Daria Price. *Presentations: Proven Techniques for Creating Presentations That Get Results.* Adams Media Corporation, 1998.

Bowman, Sharon L. *Presenting With Pizzazz.* Bowperson Publishing, 1997.

Boylan, Bob. *What's Your Point?: The 3-Step Method for Making Effective Presentations.* Adams Media Corporation, 2001.

Brody, Marjorie, and Shawn Kent. *Power Presentations: How to Connect with Your Audience and Sell Your Ideas.* John Wiley & Sons, 1992.

Brody, Marjorie. *Speaking Your Way to the Top: Making Powerful Business Presentations.* Allyn & Bacon, 1997.

Campbell, G. Michael. *Bulletproof Presentations.* Career Press, 2002.

Detz, Joan. *It's Not What You Say, It's How You Say It: Ready-to-Use Advice for Presentations, Speeches, and Other Speaking Occasions, Large and Small.* Griffin Trade Paperback, 2000.

Diresta, Diane. *Knockout Presentations: How to Deliver Your Message with Power, Punch, and Pizzazz.* Chandler House Press, 1998.

Ehrenborg, Jons, and John Mattock. *Powerful Presentations.* Kogan Page Ltd., 2001.

Endicott, Jim, and Scott W. Lee. *The Presentation Survival Skills Guide.* Distinction Publishing, 2001.

Esposito, Janet E. *In The Spotlight: Overcome Your Fear of Public Speaking and Performing.* Strong Books, 2000.

Frank, Steven. *Public Speaking: Proven Techniques for Giving Successful Talks Every Time.* Adams Media Corporation, 1999.

Gladis, Stephen D. *The Manager's Pocket Guide to Public Presentations.* Human Resource Development Press, 1999.

Gottesman, Deb, and Buzz Mauro. *Taking Center Stage: Masterful Public Speaking Using Acting Skills You Never Knew You Had.* Berkley Publishing Group, 2001.

Greenberg, David. *Simply Speaking!: The No-Sweat Way to Prepare and Deliver Presentations.* Goldleaf Publishing, 2000.

Hill, Matt. *Do It Right in Front of an Audience: A Quick-Read Presentation Skills Handbook.* The Hill Group, 2002.

Hillman, Ralph, and William D. Thompson. *Delivering Dynamic Presentations: Using Your Voice and Body for Impact.* Allyn & Bacon, 1998.

Hoff, Ron, and Barrie Maguire. *I Can See You Naked: A New Revised Edition of the National Bestseller on Making Fearless Presentations.* Andrews McMeel Publishing, 1992.

Hoff, Ron, and Barrie Maguire. *Say It in Six: How to Say Exactly What You Mean in Six Minutes or Less.* Andrews McMeel Publishing, 1996.

Hoff, Ron. *Do Not Go Naked Into Your Next Presentation: Nifty, Little Nuggets to Quiet the Nerves and Please the Crowd.* Andrews McMeel Publishing, 1997.

Holliday, Micki. *Secrets of Power Presentations: Overcome Your Fear of Public Speaking, Build Rapport and Credibility With Your Audience, Prepare and Deliver a Dynamic Presentation.* Career Press, 2000.

Jolles, Robert L. *How to Run Seminars and Workshops: Presentation Skills for Consultants, Trainers, and Teachers.* John Wiley & Sons, 2000.

Joss, Molly. *Looking Good in Presentations.* Paraglyph Publishing, 2002.

Kaye, Ellen. *Maximize Your Presentation Skills: How to Speak, Look and Act on Your Way to the Top.* Prima Publishing, 2002.

Krasne, Margo T. *Say It With Confidence: Overcoming the Mental Blocks That Keep You From Making Great Presentations & Speeches.* Warner Books, 1997.

Kushner, Malcolm, and Norman R. Augustine. *Successful Presentations for Dummies.* Hungry Minds, 1996.

Linver, Sandy, and Jim Mengert. *Speak and Get Results: The Complete Guide to Speeches and Presentations That Work in Any Business Situation.* Fireside, 1994.

Mandel, Steve. *Effective Presentation Skills: A Practical Guide for Better Speaking.* Crisp Publications, 2000.

Peoples, David A. *Presentations Plus: David Peoples' Proven Techniques* (revised edition). John Wiley & Sons, 1997.

Pike, Robert, and Arch Dave. *Dealing With Difficult Participants: 127 Practical Strategies for Minimizing Resistance and Maximizing Results in Your Presentations.* Jossey-Bass, 1997.

Pike, Robert W. *High Impact Presentations.* Provant Media, 1995.

Silberman, Mel, and Kathy Clark. *101 Ways to Make Meetings Active: Surefire Ideas to Engage Your Group.* Pfeiffer & Co, 1999.

Stettner, Morey. *Mastering Business Presentations.* The National Institute of Business Management, 2002.

Tierney, Elizabeth P. *101 Ways to Make More Effective Presentations.* Kogan Page Ltd., 1999.

Wagstaffe, James. *Romancing the Room: How to Engage Your Audience, Court Your Crowd, and Speak Successfully in Public.* Three Rivers Press, 2002.

Walters, Lilly. *Secrets of Superstar Speakers: Wisdom from the Greatest Motivators of Our Time.* McGraw-Hill Trade, 2000.

Walters, Lilly. *What to Say When You're Dying on the Platform: A Complete Resource for Speakers, Trainers, and Executives.* McGraw-Hill Trade, 1995.

Westerfield, Jude. *I Have to Give a Presentation, Now What?!: Overcome Your Fears/Using PowerPoint/Pacing Your Presentation.* Friedman/Fairfax Publishing, 2002.

Wilder, Lilyan. *Seven Steps to Fearless Speaking.* John Wiley & Sons, 1999.

Wircenski, Jerry L., and Richard L. Sullivan. "Make Every Presentation a Winner." *Info-line,* ASTD, 1986 (revised 1998).

Yate, Martin John, and Peter J. Sander. *Knock 'Em Dead Business Presentations.* Adams Media Corporation, November 2002.

Zelazny, Gene. *Say It With Presentations: How to Design and Deliver Successful Business Presentations.* McGraw-Hill Trade, 1999.

Audio Resources

Hartman, Jackie Jankovich, and Elaine A. LeMay. *Presentation Success: A Step-by-Step Approach.* South-Western College Publishing, 2000.

Smith, Debra West (reader). *Powerful Presentation Skills: How to Get a Group's Attention, Hold People's Interest and Persuade Them to Act.* CareerTrack Publications, 1998.

Sutton, Helen (reader). *Speaking Without Fear or Nervousness.* CareerTrack Publications and Fred Pryor Seminars, 1997.

Games, Openers, and Closers

Arch, Dave. *Showmanship for Presenters: 49 Proven Training Techniques from Professional Performers.* Jossey-Bass, 1999.

Arch, Dave. *Tricks for Trainers: 57 Tricks and Teasers Guaranteed to Add Magic to Your Presentation* (volume 1). Jossey-Bass, 1999.

Caroselli, Marlene. *Great Session Openers, Closers, and Energizers: Quick Activities for Warming Up Your Audience and Ending on a High Note.* McGraw-Hill Trade, 1998.

Hodgin, Michael. *1001 Humorous Illustrations for Public Speaking.* Zondervan, 1995.

Kroehnert, Gary. *101 More Training Games.* McGraw-Hill, 1999.

Newstrom, John W., and Edward Scannell. *The Big Book of Presentation Games: Wake-Em-Up Tricks, Icebreakers, and Other Fun Stuff.* McGraw-Hill Trade, 1997.

Pike, Robert, and Lynn Solem. *50 Creative Training Openers and Energizers: Innovative Ways to Start Your Training with a BANG!* Jossey-Bass, 2000.

Rose, Ed. *Presenting & Training With Magic.* McGraw-Hill Trade, 1997.

Slott, Phil. *Never Let 'em See You Sweat: A Tranquilizer For Presenters.* Alliance House Inc., 2000.

Solem, Lynn, and Robert Pike. *50 Creative Training Closers: Innovative Ways to End Your Training With IMPACT!* Jossey-Bass, 1998.

Underwood, Tom. *Wuzzles for Presenters.* Jossey-Bass, 2000.

Weissman, Jerry. *Presenting to Win: The Art of Telling Your Story.* Financial Times Prentice Hall, 2003.

PowerPoint and Other Audiovisual Help

Brandt, Richard L. *Flip Charts: How to Draw Them and How to Use Them.* Pfeiffer, 1997.

Burn, Bonnie E. *Flip Chart Power: Secrets of the Masters.* Pfeiffer, 1996.

Kearney, Lynn, and Colleen Wilder (editor). *Graphics for Presenters: Getting Your Ideas Across (50-Minute).* Crisp Publications, 1996.

Lowe, Doug. *PowerPoint 2002 for Dummies.* John Wiley & Sons, 2001.

Lucas, Robert William. *The Big Book of Flip Charts.* McGraw-Hill Trade, 1999.

McCue, Camille. *PowerPoint 2000 for Windows for Dummies Quick Reference.* John Wiley & Sons, 1999.

Nicol, Adelheid A.M., and Penny M. Pexman. *Displaying Your Findings: A Practical Guide for Presenting Figures, Posters, and Presentations.* American Psychological Association, 2003.

Wilder, Claudyne, and Jennifer Rotondo. *Point, Click & Wow!* (with CD-ROM). Jossey-Bass, 2002.

Zelazny, Gene. *Say It With Charts: The Executive's Guide to Visual Communication.* McGraw-Hill Trade, 2001.

Advanced Techniques

Dowling, Michael J., and Ellen C. Dowling. *Presenting With Style: Advanced Strategies for Superior Presentations.* iUniverse.com, 2000.

Kahrs, Till K. *Enhancing Your Presentation Skills.* iUniverse.com, 2000.

Wircenski, Jerry L., and Richard L. Sullivan. "Make Every Presentation a Winner," *Info-line,* ASTD, 1986 (revised 1998).

About the Author

■ ■

Robert J. Rosania is a vice president and delivery consultant for Manchester, a human capital management consulting firm. He is a nationally recognized training and development professional with more than 20 years' experience working with individuals and organizations to improve performance, manage change, and develop effective career management strategies.

Rosania wrote *The Credible Trainer: Create Value for Training, Get Respect for Your Ideas, and Boost Your Career* (ASTD, 2000), a book that tied for the highest rating given by *Training* magazine for books reviewed in 2001. He's also a major contributor to an ASTD series, *In Action: Improving Performance in Organizations*, and he's written articles for *Hospitals Magazine* and *Training & Development.*

In addition, he has appeared on a number of Philadelphia radio programs speaking on career development and work-life balance issues and has been a guest presenter at national meetings for the American Dietitian Association, ASTD, and the Training Directors' Forum. As an adjunct instructor he has taught psychology at Mercer County Community College, as well as leadership and motivation at Penn State University-Ogontz. Furthermore, he's appeared as a guest lecturer for the graduate program in training and development at St. Joseph's University.

Rosania earned a master of arts degree in student personnel services in higher education (counseling) from Seton Hall University and a bachelor of arts degree in psychology from the University of Dayton.

He is a member of ASTD and the Association of Career Professionals International.

Rosania lives in suburban Philadelphia with his wife, Vera Regoli, and their son, Aaron. He can be reached at brosania@aol.com or robert.rosania@manchesterus.com.

ASTD PRESS

Delivering Training and Performance Knowledge
You Will Use Today and Lead With Tomorrow

- Training Basics
- Evaluation and Return-on-Investment (ROI)
- E-Learning
- Instructional Systems Development (ISD)
- Leadership
- Career Development

ASTD Press is an internationally renowned source of insightful and practical information on workplace learning and performance topics, including training basics, evaluation and return-on-investment (ROI), instructional systems development (ISD), e-learning, leadership, and career development. You can trust that the books ASTD Press acquires, develops, edits, designs, and publishes meet the highest standards and that they reflect the most current industry practices. In addition, ASTD Press books are bottom-line oriented and geared toward immediate problem-solving application in the field.

Ordering Information: Purchase books published by ASTD Press by visiting our Website at store.astd.org or by calling 800.628.2783 or 703.683.8100.